THE FINAL EXODUS

Let My People Go

APOSTLE FREDERICK E. FRANKLIN

authorHOUSE®

AuthorHouse™ LLC
1663 Liberty Drive
Bloomington, IN 47403
www.authorhouse.com
Phone: 1-800-839-8640

Published by AuthorHouse 10/22/2013

ISBN: 978-1-4918-2847-2 (sc)
ISBN: 978-1-4918-2846-5 (e)

Library of Congress Control Number: 2013919063

CONTENTS

INTRODUCTION

"THE FINAL EXODUS" is our (47th) forty seventh Book which we have written. This is the most important and powerful Book that we have written. This Book, also, like all of our previous (46) forty six Books, was written because God told us to write it.

To say that this is the most powerful and important Book that we have written, is a very great boast in God providing us and the rest of humanity his secrets and mysteries. We say this because God has unlocked his secrets and mysteries to all of us in this Book that are truly shocking; this Book enlightens like no other book ever written, except for the Holy Bible. This Book will covert Muslims, those of the Hindu Faith, so-called Christians and others, to the truth of God's word. Maybe only understood by the so-called Christians and true saints, this Book separates the sheep from the goats.

This Book not only tells what Cain's Mark was; this Book not only breaks an historical stronghold of witchcraft off most of the inhabitants of the earth; this Book not only reveals the United States like never before; this Book not only explains why the (NRA) National Rifle Association stand on guns is as it is; this Book not only tells you God's mind regarding slavery; this Book not only reveals what God says regarding planetary travel and other planetary matters; this Book reveals God's mind on sodomy/homosexuality; this Book not only tells how to get delivered from sodomy/homosexuality; this Book not only tells how to stay delivered from sodomy/homosexuality; this Book not only tells who God hates the most on this earth and it is not sodomites/homosexuals; this Book not only tells why babies and young children are sodomites/homosexuals; this Book not only tells how to prevent babies and young children from becoming sodomites/homosexuals; this Book not only tells God's view on pets; this Book not only tells how pets are related to end times prophesy; this Book not only tells us about the roots of pornography; this Book not only addresses talking to a dead love one; this Book not only tells who the (Anti-Christ) Beast will be; this Book not only tells who the other Beast, False prophet will be; but much, much, more. This Book is very enlightening.

This Book not only let Black people know that they are Jews; this Book not only shows Black people heritage with JESUS Christ; this Book not only set Black people free; this Book not only reveals the lies that we thought to be trues and facts; but much, much, more. This Book is very enlightening.

This Book tells how God showed us that only (148,000) one hundred forty eight thousand souls will be saved in the United States. This Book provides an answer and solution that God has provided for only (148,000) one hundred forty eight thousand souls being saved in the United States. This Book shows how Capitalism work in the United States and God's people, Black Jews, to the success of it. This Book tells who contribute over a trillion dollars to the United States' economy per year. This Book tells who will be in the Great Exodus. This Book tells how many will be in the Great Exodus. This Book tells where the Great Exodus will leave from. This Book tells where the Great Exodus will go to. This Book points out the idol God worship in the United States; unknowingly to the worshippers. God tells of the Great Depression that will occur and how God will use it. This Book provides God's purpose for the judgment associated with the Sounding of the Fifth Trumpet. God in this Book tells why the plague will last for (5) five months. Much, much, more, this Book provides through revelation given to us directly from God and through God's written word. This Book is very enlightening.

You will agree with us, no other Book ever written is as enlightening as this Book, with the exception of the Holy Bible. This Book is wonderfully informative. This Book will turn the world upside down. God will use this Book to get all of our Books distributed throughout the earth. Although we are little known at this time, this Book will make us known by all the world; saved and non-saved. This Book will facilitate Apostle Frederick E. Franklin establishing God's end times Church. This

CHAPTER 1

<u>What Was Cain's Mark?</u>

(THE FINAL EXODUS)

This Chapter is an edited edition/rendering of our Book "What Was Cain's Mark?" The editing in no way changes any content of that Book. The editing was only done to adapt that Book for this Chapter and this Book.

This was our (46th) forty-sixth Book which we had written. Before we began to write this Book, we had much prayer to God concerning the writing of it. We believed that God had told us to write it several times, in a span of over a years' time, but we were not sure. We had not received the confirmation from God to write that we were looking for. We had asked God to confirm to us in a vision or dream.

We have written some very controversial books. In fact, most to all of them have had this status. Our books have been so controversial, that when we first tried to get our (1st) first Book published, no one would touch it. We tried different publishers, but no one would touch it. Finally we thought that we had found a publisher, but after having said they would publish it, they later on refused to. After all of our failed attempts to get the

Book published, we received, "out of the clear blue", in the next week a letter in the mail from a publisher saying that they would publish our Book no matter how controversial it might be. We knew it had to be God. God had someone to send this promotion to us.

Although our previous books which we accomplished to publish have been controversial, this present Book makes them seem non-controversial in comparison. It is like comparing a mole hill to a mountain. It is like comparing a midget to a professional basketball player who plays center. To satisfy your taste for sweetness, like comparing vinegar to a sun ripened grape.

Due to the extreme level of controversy to what we believed that God was telling us to write, we had to be absolutely sure that it was God telling us to write. We had to be sure, as you will understand as you read this Book.

Finally, on September 23, 2013, we received this confirmation. God told us, indisputably, that we should write this Book. We had already written everything in the Book except this statement of God's confirmation for us to write it. So, when we received the confirmation, that we were looking for, we merely inserted this confirmation into the Book to get it published.

God let us know that for the publishing of this Book is one of the reasons he had the (1st) First Amendment to be added to the United States' Constitution. The (1st) First Amendment is the Freedom of Speech.

In the beginning of the history of Mankind, after God made Adam and Eve, their first child was born. Their first born was a man child and his name was Cain.

Genesis Ch. 2, V. 7
"And the LORD formed man from the dust of the ground, and breathed into his nostrils the breath of life; and he became a living soul."

You might ask at this point, why did God have to form this man from the dust of the ground, when earlier Scriptures indicated that God created all men and women on the six day? We are ready and very anxious to answer the question concerning forming man from the dust, since the Devil, Satan, has sent out his ministers to lie so grievously concerning this matter. The Devil, Satan, has his ministers saying that Adam and his eventual wife, Eve, were not the first people on this earth. That they were not the beginning of Mankind. Satan uses these lying ministers to pervert the word of God like no others have ever done. There are two of these ministers of Satan that has a worldwide television program. They have deceived and are deceiving all over the world. Satan through these two ministers, also, say that Cain was not Adam's son. They say that Eve committed adultery with Satan. They say that Satan is Cain's father. What stupidity! What ignorance! What perversion! What disregard of God's word! What lies!

Before we go any further, let us clear up this lie since we are talking about man's creation. This is straying away from the main subject, but let us address this matter first.

<u>Genesis Ch. 1, Vs. 26-28</u>
"And God said, Let us make man in our image, after our likeness: and let them have dominion over the fish of the sea, and over the fowl of the air, and over the cattle, and over every creeping thing that creepeth upon the earth. So God created man in his own image, in the image of God created he him; male and female created he them. And God blessed them, and God said unto them, Be fruitful and multiply, and replenish the earth, and subdue it . . ."

First of all let us point this out. In the above Scripture, God said, "Be fruitful and multiply, and replenish the earth . . ." When God created male and female, he created all of the human creation that would ever be. They were spirit beings in heaven and not on this earth. They were in heaven awaiting their appointed time to be born and put on this earth; like any who have not been conceived. Those that are put on earth were to be fruitful, multiply and replenish the earth. "Replenish" means replacing those who die. The spiritual beings created on the six day cannot die. Spirits do not die. Now let us go further.

Unlike what most, nearly all, of the "trinity" believers assert, the Father was not talking to the Son and to the Holy Ghost/Spirit when God said in the above Scriptures "Let us make man in our image and after our likeness". The Father was talking to the angels. When in the beginning God created the heaven and the earth, the angels were created then. Angels did not have to grow up. They were made from the very beginning what they would be. God, himself, told me that he was talking to the angels. Now let us get back on track. Let us get back to the main subject.

God indeed created mankind on the six day; these were spiritual beings created of mankind. This spiritual creation was done in heaven by God; they were and are held in heaven until their appointed time to be born in the flesh. They were and are not on earth until that time. Adam and Eve were the first to receive their earthly bodies. What you must understand, that all things that are natural was first spiritual. God first spoke them to be in the spirit realm and they that were to be earthly, was manifested in the natural. This is further illustrated in Genesis Chapter 2, Verse 19. God had already created creeping things, but here in Genesis Chapter 2, Verse19, it says that God formed them from the ground.

Genesis Ch. 1, Vs. 23-25

"And the evening and the morning were the fifth day. And God said, Let the earth bring forth the living creature after his kind, cattle, and creeping thing, and beast of the earth after his kind: and it was so. And God made the beast of the earth after his kind, and cattle after his kind, and every creeping thing that creepeth the earth after his kind: and saw that it was good."

Now far after this time, look at what the Scripture says.

Genesis Ch. 2, V.19

"And out of the ground the LORD formed every beast of the field, and every fowl of the air; and brought them to Adam . . ."

When man that will be saved die, his soul returns to God. If you are not saved your soul goes to hell.

Ecclessiastes Ch. 12, V. 7

"Then shall the dust return to the earth as it was: and the spirit shall return unto God who gave it."

Remember, understand, your soul is spirit.

Before JESUS' death, burial and resurrection, those that died went into a place that was in the center of the earth. If you were saved, you went to a place called paradise. If you were not saved, lost, the place where you went was across from paradise called hell. Hell is yet where those who die go who are not saved. For those who are saved since JESUS' resurrection, they go into heaven where God is and where the souls/spirits that have not been born are. As the Scriptures indicate, upon JESUS' resurrection, the souls that were in paradise in the center of the earth came out from there.

Matthew Ch. 27, Vs. 50-53
"Jesus, when he had cried again with a loud voice, yield up the ghost. And behold, the vail of the temple was rent in twain from the top to the bottom; and the earth did quake, and the rocks rent; And the graves were opened; and many bodies of saints which slept arose, after his resurrection, and went into the city, and appeared unto many."

Luke Ch. 16, Vs. 19-26
"There was a certain rich man . . . And there was a certain beggar named Lazarus . . . And it came to pass that the beggar died, and was carried by the angels into Abraham's bosom: the rich man also died, and was buried: And in hell he lifted up his eyes, being in torments, and seeth Abraham afar off, and Lazarus in his bosom. And he cried and said, Father Abraham,

have mercy on me, and send Lazarus, that he may dip the tip of his finger in water, and cool my tongue; for I am tormented in this flame. But Abraham said, Son, remember that thou in thy lifetime receivedst thy good things, and likewise Lazarus evil things: but now he is comforted, and thou art tormented. And besides all this, between us and you there is a great gulf fixed: so that they which would pass from hence to you cannot; neither can they pass to us, that would come from thence."

Let us get back to the main subject. Let us get back to the mark of Cain. Let us get back to Adam and Eve. We have shown that God made Adam from the dust of the ground to be the first man upon the earth. God also made Eve to be the first woman. What you must remember that all things that are natural was first spiritual. God spoke them to be in the spirit and they were then manifested in the natural.

Genesis Ch. 2, Vs. 18,21-25
"And the LORD said, It is not good that the man should be alone; I will make him a help meet for him. And the LORD caused a deep sleep to fall upon Adam, and he slept: and he took one of his ribs, and closed up the flesh thereof; And the rib, which the LORD God had taken from the man, made he a woman, and brought her unto the man. And Adam said, This is bone of my bones, and flesh of my flesh: she shall be called Woman, because

she was taken out of Man. Therefore shall a man leave his father and mother, and shall cleave to his wife: and they shall be one flesh."

Genesis Ch. 3, V. 30
"And Adam called his wife's name Eve; because she was the mother of all living."

After God had eventually kicked Adam and Eve out of the Garden of Eden because Eve was deceived by Satan and Adam disobeyed God, they, Adam and Eve, eventually had a son called Cain.

Genesis Ch. 4, V. 1
"And Adam knew Eve his wife; and she conceived and bare Cain, and said, I have gotten a man from the LORD."

If Cain had been the son of Satan, as the lying ministers of Satan say, then Eve would not have said, "I have gotten a man from the LORD". To believe otherwise, you must believe that the Scriptures of the Holy Bible is a lie.

These lying ministers of Satan that we mentioned earlier, perverts the word of God in even other ways also. Truly outrageous lies. They even say that you do not burn if you go to hell. They say that the loving God would not allow it to be so; no matter what the Scriptures say.

9

These lying ministers are not saved; they are not born of God. If you are not born of God, born again, you go to hell. No wonder they want to believe that you do not burn when you go to hell. These lying ministers rely on some books of men interpretation of the Holy Scriptures as if the interpreters were God. They claim that in some Greek or Arab or some other language, it says such and such of the Scriptures. Who will you believe, the Holy Scriptures of the Holy Bible or them. They cannot even understand Scriptures written in English, their native tongue, but they want you to believe that they are so intelligent to understand the Scriptures in a language that is not their own. God has warned of these perverters in his word through Apostle Paul.

II Timothy Ch. 3, Vs. 5 & 7
"Having a form of godliness, but denying the power thereof: from such turn away. Ever learning and never able to come to the knowledge of the truth."

After Adam and Eve gave birth to Cain, they also gave birth to a second Son called Abel.

Genesis Ch. 4, V. 2
"And she again bare his brother Abel. And Abel was a keeper of sheep, but Cain was a tiller of the ground."

The Holy Scriptures tell us that Cain would eventually kill his brother Abel because of envy and jealousy.

These are the two sins that Lucifer, later to be called Satan, had that caused him to lose his place, power and authority in heaven.

Genesis Ch. 4, Vs. 3-12

"And in the process of time it came to pass, that Cain brought of the fruit of the ground an offering unto the LORD. And Abel, he also brought of the firstlings of his flock and of the fat thereof. And the LORD had respect unto Abel and to his offering: But unto Cain and to his offering he had not respect. And Cain was very wroth, and his countenance fell. And the LORD said unto Cain, Why art thou wroth? And why is thy countenance fallen? If thou doest well, shall thou not be accepted? And if thou doest not well, sin lieth at the door. And unto thee shall be his desire, and thou shall rule over him. And Cain talked with Abel his brother: and it came to pass, when they were in the field, that Cain rose up against Abel his brother, and slew him."

This was, of course, the first murder upon the earth of countless multitudes to come. So here in the above Scriptures we can see a distinguishing trait of the off spring of Cain. They would be murderers and because of their envy and jealousy, they will strive to rule over other human beings. We have written about this in our previous books. God told us that racism is the sin of envy and jealousy. Refer to our Books:

1. "Words From God, By God Appearing To Us Or Just Talking To Us, For The End Times"
2. "God Said Black People In The United States Are Jews"

God also shows us in the Scriptures other distinguishing traits of Cain's off spring.

<u>Genesis Ch. 4, Vs. 9-12</u>
"And the LORD said unto Cain, Where is Abel thy brother? And he said, I know not: Am I my brother's keeper? And he said, What has thou done? The voice of thy brother's blood crieth unto me from the ground. And now art thou cursed from the earth, which hath opened her mouth to received thy brother's blood from thy hand. When thou tillest the ground, it shall not henceforth yield unto thee her strength. A fugitive and vagabond shalt thou be in the earth."

The above Scriptures indicate that the off spring of Cain would readily tell a lie; lying even to and before God himself. Also, the above Scriptures indicate that the off spring of Cain would be lawless, even a fugitive and vagabond. A vagabond is a person that has no permanent land given by God. The person or people would go from place to place, location to location, across the earth. They would not be as China, India or some others. They would try to take over the earth, such as, Alexander The Great, the Roman Empire, the British

Empire, Adolph Hitler and the United States. This is what the Scripture of Revelation Chapter 6, Verse 2, is referring to, says God.

Revelation Ch. 6, V. 2

"And I saw, and behold a white horse: and he that sat on him had a bow; a crown was given to him: and he went forth conquering, and to conquer."

Unlike what Satan's ministers say, the above Scripture is not talking about the so-called Anti-Christ, the Beast. Refer to our Books:

1.   "The Name Of The (Anti-Christ) Beast And 666 Identification"
2.   "What God Is Now Telling His Prophets About The End Times"

The earlier given Scriptures of Genesis Chapter 4, Verses 9-12, also, indicate that the off spring of Cain will not have any land of their own by inheritance and any that they have will be stolen or taken from others.

Another important trait or characteristic of Cain's off spring is the indicated relationship that they would have with God.

Genesis Ch. 4, Vs. 14 & 16

"Behold, thou had driven me out this day from the face of the earth; and from thy face shall I be hid . . . And Cain went out from the presence of the LORD . . ."

The above Scriptures indicate that Cain and his off spring would be in idolatry. If God is not man's God, then Satan would be his god. Man's is a religious being. Man either worships God or Satan.

John Ch. 8, Vs. 42-44

"Jesus said unto them, If God were your Father, ye would love me: for I proceeded forth and come from God; neither came I of myself, but he sent me. Why do ye not understand my speech? even because ye cannot hear my words. Ye are of your father the devil, and the lusts of your father ye will do. He was a murderer from the beginning, and abode not in the truth, because there is no truth in him. When he speaketh a lie, he speaketh of his own: for he is a liar, and the father of it."

The above statements and Scriptures are why God said what he said to my wife, Prophetess Sylvia Franklin. We will tell you later what God said. It is shocking. Based on all we have read, heard and seen in the different media outlets, it would seem impossible.

There are yet other traits that the Scriptures reveal to us about the offspring's of Cain. You might wonder, where did Cain get a wife from? Cain's wife was a daughter of Adam and Eve. So says God.

Genesis Ch. 4, Vs. 13-15

"And Cain said unto the LORD, My punishment is more than I can bear, Behold, thou hast driven me out this day from the face of the earth; and from thy face shall I be hid; and I shall be a fugitive and vagabond in the earth; and it shall come to pass, that every one that findeth me shall slay me. And the LORD said unto him, Therefore whosoever slayeth Cain, vengeance shall be taken on him sevenfold. And the LORD set a mark upon Cain, lest any finding him should kill him."

This "mark upon Cain" would have to be something that was easily to be recognized by others. If the vengeance of God would come upon you sevenfold for killing Cain, then the mark would have to be readily and easily seen.

The anthropologist have said that the first man was found in Africa. An anthropologist is one who through science studies the origin of man who does not believe the Holy Scriptures/Bible. The anthropologist's scientific conclusion seems to make sense. There is no mixture of people that will produce a Black man who has not been with another ethnic. There is no mixture that will get the hair. There is no mixture that will get the facial features. So then, Adam and Eve were Black.

The mark of Cain then would have to be indisputable. It would have to be something that would make Cain stand out from everyone else. Cain could not look like Adam. Cain could not look like Eve. Cain could like Adam's and Eve's third son Seth. There had to be something about Cain that was different from these three Black people. God revealed to us that this difference was that Cain's curse by him was a curse in his pigmentation of his skin. His skin was bleached of its color. His skin was made pale. So says God. So, Cain looked like what we call white people, Caucasians. Cain was the first Caucasian. This way everyone could easily and readily recognize Cain. This curse by God left Cain's face and skin pale; unlike the Black Adam, Eve and Seth. SO SAYS GOD!

There are further traits or characteristics about Cain's off spring that the Scriptures reveal.

Genesis Ch. 4, Vs. 17-19 & 22

"And Cain knew his wife, and she conceived, and bare Enoch: and he build a city, after the name of his son, Enoch. And unto Enoch was born Irad: and Irad begat Mehujael, and Mehujael begat Methusael: and Methusael begat Lamech. And Lamech took upon him two wives: the name of one was Adah, and the name of the other Zillah. And Zillah, she also bare Tubal-cain, an instructor of every artificer in brass and iron . . ."

The above Scriptures indicate that the off spring of Cain would master the use of brass and iron. Brass and iron were the beginning of the weapons to kill other people. The Scriptures above also pins down a name that can be traced to other places in the Holy Scriptures/Bible, "Tubal-cain".

Noah's son Japhet married the daughter of Cain's off spring. Japhet's line can be traced to the Europeans. Also, we see Tubal of "Tubal-cain" mentioned in the Holy Scriptures in the Book of Ezekiel.

Genesis Ch. 10, V. 2
"The sons of Japheth; Gomer, and Magog, and Madia, and Javan, and Tubal, and Meshech, and Tiras."

Ezekiel Ch. 38, Vs. 2 & 3
"Son of man, set thy face against Gog, the land of Magog, the chief prince of Meshech and Tubal, and prophesy against him, And say, Thus saith the LORD GOD; Behold, I am against thee, O Gog, the chief prince of Meshech and Tubal . . ."

Magog is called in these days/times Russia. Gog is the leader of Russia.

We see that Tubal and other off spring of Cain were slave owners. Where have we heard of this before?

Ezekiel Ch. 27, V.13
"Javan, Tubal, Meshech, they were thy merchants: they traded the persons of men and vessels of brass in thy market."

There has not been since the days of Egypt of old that a people were known for slave trading, except for the Europeans. These certain people were called the enemies of God's people.

Genesis Ch. 22, V. 17
"That in blessing I will bless thee, and in multiplying I will multiply thy seed as the stars of the heaven, and as the sand which is upon the sea shore; and thy seed shall possess the gate of his enemies . . ."

Deuteronomy Ch. 28, V.68
"And the LORD shall bring thee into Egypt again with ships, by the way whereof I spake and there ye shall be sold unto your enemies for bondmen and bondwomen, and no man shall buy you."

Egypt in the above Scripture is referring to the United States. The United States in the Holy Scriptures of the Holy Bible is referred to as:

1.   Egypt
2.   Sodom
3.   The Great City

4.   Babylon The Great/The Great Babylon/ Babylon
5.   Harlot
6.   Whore
7.   Mystery
8.   The Mother Of Harlots
9.   Abominations Of The Earth
10. Woman

As we have written in other of our books, God himself told me that the United States is Babylon The Great. I will again testify of this revelation. God gave me a dream. In the dream, God and I were side by side. God was on the left of me. We were up high looking down on the earth. I do not know whether we were in the first heaven, second heaven or third heaven. All of a sudden God opened up a very large and very thick Book to me. This I understood somehow, through revelation to my mine, as God told me, was the Book that contained every event of the history of mankind. God then opened the Book to the back part of the back of the Book. As God then turned the pages toward the end of the Book, the written words on the page of the Book became a vision. We were looking down on the vision. God let me know that He was showing me the future. The vision was about the size of a football field; about (100) one hundred yards long and (50) fifty hundred yards wide. I will not tell you everything that God showed me. I will, however, tell you what God told me and showed me as it relates to showing that the United States is Babylon The Great. As God turned the page of future events, I saw missiles flying through the air. These missiles were arrayed in pattern like as fowl flying through the sky in winter migration. These missiles, God let me know that they were of the nuclear and poison gas variety. As God then again turned the page, the written words again became a large vision that we were looking down on. In this vision of the future God showed me fire and explosion happening somewhere on earth. Again as God turned the page and the corresponding vision appeared, there in the vision were large fowl somewhere on the earth. These fowl were nasty. They were vomiting. They were filthy. They looked retarded and deformed. God told me to open up my Bible of the Holy Scriptures and turn to Revelation Chapter 18 and read.

Revelation Ch. 18, Vs. 1-2

"And after these things I saw another angel come down from heaven, having great power; and the earth was lightened with his glory. And he cried mightily with a strong voice, saying, Babylon the great is fallen, is fallen, and is become the habitation of devils, and the hold of every fowl spirit, and a cage of every unclean and hateful bird."

God told me after reading the above Scriptures, that the "cage of every unclean and hateful" were those nasty, filthy, vomiting and retarded and deformed fowl that I saw in the vision. God, also, said that these fowl were in the condition they were in because of the missiles that I saw in the vision. God said that these fowl were like this because they were contaminated by the nuclear and poison gas bombing. This bombing, God told me, was the fire and explosions that I saw in the vision. God told me that this fire and explosion was happening in the United States and that the United States is Babylon the Great.

God also showed me in the visions during this time, how many would be saved in the United States. As God turned the page, a still vision appeared. This still vision was also about the length of a football field. The still vision was merely a number. It was the number of souls that will be saved in the United States. I thought that my eyes were deceiving me. I was shocked. It was amazing. I was astounded. I saw the exact number of those who would be saved in the United States. I saw the exact number that would be in the First Resurrection, the so-called rapture. The number was not (148,000,000) one hundred forty eight million. The number was not (14,800,000) fourteen million eight hundred thousand. The number was not (1,480,000) million four hundred eighty thousand. The number, shockingly, was (148,000) one hundred forty eight thousand. Yes, only (148,000) one hundred forty eight thousand souls will be saved in the United States. The United States, the so-called

Christian nation; a nation of over (300,000,000) three hundred million. Refer to our Books:

1. "United States In The Bible"
2. "The Judgment Of The United States"
3. "Words From God, By God Appearing To Us Or Just Talking To Us, For The End Times"
4. "The Ten Horns Of The Books Of Daniel And Revelation"

Remember this regarding Deuteronomy Chapter 28, Verse 68, in Egypt of old, the slaves, God's people, the children of Israel, did not go there by way of ships.

Deuteronomy Ch. 28, V. 68
"And the LORD shall bring thee into Egypt again with ships, by the way whereof I spake and ye shall be sold unto your enemies for bondmen and bondwomen . . ."

Revelation Ch. 17, Vs. 4 & 5
"And the woman was arrayed in purple and scarlet colour, and decked with gold and precious stones and pearls, having a golden cup in her hand full of abominations and filthiness of her fornication: And upon her head was a name written, MYSTERY, BABYLON THE GREAT, THE MOTHER OF HARLOTS AND ABOMINATIONS OF THE EARTH."

Revelation Ch. 17, V. 18

"And the woman which thou sawest is that great city, which reigneth over the kings of the earth."

Revelation Ch. 18, Vs. 8-10

"Therefore shall her plagues come in one day, death, and mourning, and famine; and she shall be utterly burnt with fire: for strong is the LORD God who judgeth her. And the kings of the earth, who have committed fornication and lived deliciously with her, shall bewail her, and lament for her, when they shall see the smoke of her burning. Standing afar off for the fear of her torment, saying, Alas, alas, that great city Babylon, that mighty city! For in one hour is thy judgment come."

In the above Scriptures, they were standing far off for fear of contamination of the nuclear and poison gas bombing.

Revelation Ch. 18, Vs. 16-18

". . . Alas, alas, that great city . . . For in one hour so great riches has come to nought. And every shipmaster, and all the company in ships, and sailers, and as many as trade by sea, stood afar off, And cried when they saw the smoke of her burning, saying, What city is like unto this great city?"

Revelation Ch. 18, V. 21

"And a mighty angel took up a great millstone, and cast it unto the sea, saying, Thus with violence shall that great city Babylon be thrown down, and shall not be found no more at all."

Revelation Ch. 11, Vs. 3,7 & 8

"And I will give power unto my two witnesses . . . And when they shall have finished their testimony, the beast . . . shall . . . kill them. And their dead bodies shall lie in the street of the great city, which spiritually is called Sodom and Egypt, where also our Lord was crucified."

Many and most have thought, incorrectly, that the two witnesses will be killed in Jerusalem because of the part of the above Scripture which say "where also our Lord was crucified". The correct interpretation is that the two witnesses' "dead bodies shall lie in the street", just as the Lord was crucified in the street. So, therefore, the Great City is also called Sodom; which is also called Egypt; which is also called Babylon The Great; which is the United States of America.

Deuteronomy Ch. 28, V. 68

"And the Lord shall bring thee into Egypt again with ships, by the way thereof I spake unto thee, thou shall see it no more again: and there ye shall be sold unto your enemies for bondmen and bond women, and no man shall buy you."

So, we see that God told us before, even during Moses' day, that Tubal and others of the off spring of Cain, would have slaves of God's people in the United States.

Ezekiel Ch. 27, V. 13
"Javan, Tubal, and Meshech, they were thy merchants: they traded the persons of men, and vessels of brass and iron in thy markets."

Another indication that Babylon the Great is the United States can be seen in the Scriptures reference to Babylon the Great as having slaves in the latter days.

Revelation Ch. 18, Vs. 10-13
". . . that great city Babylon . . . the merchants of the earth shall weep and mourn over her; for no man buyeth their merchandise any more: The merchandise of . . . slaves . . ."

Some of Cain's off spring, white folks, pale people, have said that God is not against slavery to justify their slavery efforts across the earth. They have said that God meant it to be so that Black People are to be slaves. They have also said that God did not say anything against slavery in his word. All of the above in this paragraph is not true concerning God. Not only is it shown not to be true through God bringing judgment against the perpetrators of slavery, but also God even says in his word that the benefits that might be gain from slavery is an abomination to him.

<u>Deuteronomy Ch. 23, V. 18</u>
"Thou shall not bring the hire of a whore, or the price of a dog into the house of the LORD thy God for any vow: for even both these are abomination unto the LORD thy God."

The "price of a dog" in the above Scripture is referring to a person being sold as a slave; even a gentile being sold as a slave. This means that any of the riches incurred by white people having slaves is an abomination to God. God does not want your tithes and offerings resulting from your benefit of slavery. If your tithes and offerings are abominations to God, so are you an abomination to God. No wonder why so very few white people will be saved, will be in the first resurrection, the so-called rapture. So says God. Here is the seemingly impossible based on the media propaganda that we said we would tell you. God told my wife, Prophetess Sylvia Franklin, in around the Year of 2009, that there were NO WHITE PEOPLE SAVED IN BIBLICAL TIMES.

Another reference to God being against slavery is also shown in the Book of Proverbs of the Holy Scriptures/ Bible. The Book of Proverbs was written by the wises man who had ever lived at that time. Not only that, Proverbs were given by the creator of wisdom, the Almighty God, the Creator of all things.

Proverbs Ch. 16, V. 26
"He that laboureth laboureth for himself; for his mouth craveth it of him."

Here in the above Scripture God says that a man's work is to benefit him. A man's labor is primarily for his own benefit and not to benefit another, such as, a slave master. God, therefore, denounces slavery.

The lying ministers of Satan mentioned earlier and some other lying ministers of Satan, say that the children of Israel were and are the white people, Caucasians. This can very easily be shown to be a lie. Not only is this shown to be a lie of what God told my wife, Prophetess Sylvia Franklin, when God said that no white people were saved during Biblical times, but it also can be shown to be a lie in other ways.

When the children of Israel came out of Egypt it was about (3,000,000) three million of them. If we consider the death of the children of Israel due to the judgment of God in the wilderness before they came to the promise land, that number was significant, but not relative to the total number of the children of Israel. So consider that number, plus God said that no man over the age of twenty would enter into the promise land; until they all died of natural death or the judgment of God. So, therefore, the natural state of things were happening. People were dying and people being born.

Understand/Remember, that when the children of Israel went out from Egypt, there was not one feeble among them.

Exodus Ch. 15, V. 26
". . . for I am the LORD that healeth thee."

Deuteronomy Ch. 29, V. 5
"And I have led you forty years in the wilderness: your clothes are not waxen old upon you and thy shoe is not waxen old upon thy foot."

Deuteronomy Ch. 34, V. 7
"And Moses was an hundred and twenty years old when he died: his eye was not dim, nor his natural force abated."

Psalm 105, Vs. 36-37
"He smote also all the firstborn in their land, the chief of all their strength. He brought them forth also with silver and gold: and there was not one feeble person among their tribes."

The children of Israel were in good health when they went out of Egypt; all of them. This also indicate that they were all in good health in the (40) forty years in the wilderness; except for God's judgment of the snake bites.

For simplification of calculation, using very conservative figures, let us just assume that when the children of Israel went into the promise land after (40) forty years, that the number of them were yet only (3,000,000) three million. If we assume that out of the (3,000,000) three million of the children of Israel, half were females. After about (20) twenty years, all of these women would be of child bearing age. Understand this, the children of Israel had large families. Out of (3,000,000) of the children of Israel, we can assume that half of them were females which equals 1,500,000 females. Let us assume a conservative 5 children for each family; assume after about 20 years all the females leaving out of Egypt would be of child bearing age; assume only half were not too old to have children which would be 750,000 women; then

$750,000 \times 5 + 3,000,000 =$

$3,750,000 + 3,000,000 =$ <u>6,750,000 children of Israel after just 20 years.</u>

Assume half are women of the 6,750,000, then there would be 3,375,000 women. Assume only half bore children which would be 1,687,500 women; then

1,687,500 x 5 + 6,750,000 =

8,437,500 + 6,750,000 = 15,187,500 children of Israel after 40 years.

Now assume that only half of the adult population will be living after 20 years;

Assume half are women of the 15,187,500, then there would be about 7,500,000 women; assume half of that number bore children; then there would be 3,750,000 child bearing women; half of the adult population being dead after 20 years would leave 7,500,000; then

7,500,000 x 5 + 7,500,000 =

37,500,000 + 7,500,000 = 45,100,000 children after just 60 years.

Assume half are women of the 45,100,000, then there would be about 22,500,000 women. Assume half of that number bore children; then there would be 11,250,000 child bearing women; half of the adult population being dead after 20 years would leave 22,100,000; then

11,250,000 x 5 + 22,100,000 =

56,250,000 + 22,100,000 = <u>78,350,000 children of Israel after just 80 years.</u>

Assume half are women of the 78,350,000, then there would be 39,175,000 females. Assume half of that number bore children; then there would be 18,585,000 child bearing women; half of the adult population being dead after 20 years would leave 39,175,000; then

18,585,000 x 5 + 39,175,000 =

92,925,000 + 39,175,000 = <u>132,100,000 children of Israel after just 100 years.</u>

Assume half are females of the 132,100,000, then there would be about 66,000,000 females. Assume half of that number bore children; then there would be 33,000,000 child bearing women; half of the adult population being dead after 20 years would leave 66,000,000; then

33,000,000 x 5 + 66,000,000 =

165,000,000 + 66,000,000 = <u>231,000,000 children of Israel after just 120 years.</u>

Assume half are females of the 231,000,000, then there would be 115,500,000 females. Assume half of that number bore children; then there would be 57,750,000 children bearing women; half of the adult population being dead after 20 years would leave 115,500,000; then

57,750,000 x 5 + 115,500,000 =

288,750,000 + 115,500,000 = 404,250,000 children of Israel after just 140 years.

Assume half are females of the 404,250,000, then there would be 202,125,000 females. Assume half of that number bore children; then there would be 101,075,000 child bearing women; half of the adult population being dead after 20 years would leave 202,125,000; then

101,075,000 x 5 + 202,125,000 =

505,375,000 + 202,125,000 = 707,500,000 children of Israel after just 160 years.

Now this is not an exact number, but it gives you an idea. This, however, let you know that the around (500,000,000) five hundred million, white people that is now on the earth, could not be the children of Israel. After just a (160) one hundred sixty years after the children Israel came out of the wilderness to go into the promise land, there were more of the children of Israel than it is of all white people, pale people, Caucasians, that is now on the earth. Also, God said that with the children of Israel, that he would increase their numbers to a very great amount. Being in the minority as the Caucasians are, does not line up with what God said.

Genesis Ch. 22, V. 17
"That in blessing I will bless thee, and in multiplying I will multiply thy seed as the stars of the heaven, and as the sand which is upon the sea shore . . ."

Therefore, we have proved that those lying ministers of Satan who say that the white people, Caucasians, pale people, of Europe are the children of Israel is a lie. A flat out lie!

The murdering spirit of Cain's off spring, white people, pale people, is a prevailing life style with this people. They have exported their terror throughout the earth.

Ezekiel Ch. 32, V. 26
"There is Meshech, Tubal, and all her multitude: her graves are round him: all of them uncircumcised, slain by the sword, though they caused their terror in the land of the living."

This murdering by the off spring of Cain, pale people, white people, was establish from the very beginning. Not only was Cain himself the first to commit murder, but the second murder on this earth was committed by Cain's off spring, pale people, white people.

Genesis Ch. 4, Vs. 23 & 24

"And Lamech said unto his wives, Adah and Zillah, hear my voice; ye wives of Lamech, hearken to my speech: for I have slain a man to my wounding, and a young man to my hurt. If Cain shall be avenged sevenfold, truly Lamech seventy and sevenfold."

You might wonder, why did God tell Cain that if anyone would kill him, they would suffer a sevenfold punishment. God himself threatened mankind with a sevenfold judgment.

Genesis Ch. 4, V. 15

"And the LORD said unto him, Therefore whosoever slayeth Cain, vengeance shall be taken on him sevenfold. And the LORD set a mark upon Cain lest any finding him should kill him."

God needed such as Cain in a similar way that JESUS needed Judas Iscariot. If Cain had been killed then the Plan of God for Mankind could not be completed.

John Ch. 6, Vs. 70 &71

"Jesus answered them, Have not I chosen you twelve, and one of you is a devil? He spake of Judas Iscariot the son of Simon: for he it was that should betray him, being one of the twelve."

Isaiah Ch. 45, V. 7
"I formed the light, and create darkness: I make peace, and create evil: I the LORD do all these things."

You can see God using the evil of this world through his use of the (Anti-Christ) Beast. God says that he will use the (Anti-Christ) Beast to do his will.

Revelation Ch. 17, Vs. 16-17
"And the ten horns which thou sawest upon the beast, these shall hate the whore, and shall make her desolate and naked, and shall eat her flesh, and burn her with fire. For God hath put in their hearts to fulfill his will, and to agree, and to give their kingdom unto the beast, until the words of God shall be fulfilled."

God therefore needed such as Cain. Looking down through the history of Mankind, God could see how a murderer would be necessary to carry out his Plan for Mankind. God could see that such a people of the off spring of Cain, pale people, white people, having Cain's attributes would be essential for God's Plan to redeem Mankind.

Right now in the United States the spirit of Cain is dominating the News and Congressional action and discourse. This murdering spirit of Cain has a strong anchor with the (NRA) National Rifle Association. The discourse by the NRA to defend having weapons of mass murder seems unbelievable to those of us who are sane. Only a heathen and barbaric people would defend arming the general population with these murdering machines. The spirit of Cain has truly reached its height in the United States. Making it easy to butcher another human being is what that is being argued. How barbaric is this?

Also, the spirit of Cain is on full display in the United States massive military complex. The United States spending on its military is more than the next (10) ten largest militaries in the world.

Even as we write this Book, April 15, 2013, the murdering spirit of Cain is on dramatic and full display. We are referring to the bombing in the City of Boston, Massachusetts. Boston is a famous city in the United States. It is known worldwide for many things. Boston is known for its historical and political importance in the United States. Boston is also known worldwide for its athletic endeavors, among them are:

1. Boston Celtics Professional Basketball Team;
2. Boston Red Sox Professional Baseball Team;
3. Boston Bruins Professional Hockey Team;
4. Boston Marathon

The Boston Marathon, however, might be what Boston is known for from now on. This is because while we are writing this Book, during the time of the Boston Marathon, there were two bombings. The bombings were about (15) fifteen seconds apart. There were (3) three people killed and about (280) two hundred and eighty people who were wounded. Among the number that were killed and injured were children. This happened at a time when the whole world was watching the Boston Marathon. The Marathon had participants from all over the world.

The slaughter of the citizens was and is not a rarity in the United States. As of April 15, 2013, there have been approaching (4,000) four thousand murders in the United States, for this year. Over (30,000) thirty thousand people are killed every year in the United States. This is more than half of the people that were killed of the United States in the Vietnam War. Bye the way, in that murderous war, that was unprovoked, the United States killed over a million people. I ask you, is the spirit of Cain live and well in the United States? Bye the way, less we forget, the United States as a country, was established by murdering the original inhabitants, the Indians, of this land.

God told me several years ago, that guns have evil spirits associated with them. The guns were made to kill another person, therefore, Satan and the evil spirits have possessed these weapons of murder. You can actually feel the spirits associated with them. As soon as you pick up a gun, an evil spirit comes upon you. God said to me that guns are Satanic and demonic. That is why it is so easy to kill when you have a gun in your hand. That is why the (NRA) National Rifle Association and the gun manufacturers seem so evil. God said it! I remember when I was a young man, a teenager, my first cousin and I were hunting. We were in a thick wooded area in a place/community called Dawes in Mobile, Alabama here in the United States. We had got separated while hunting. I called out for my cousin to see where he was. Well, I later saw him, but he did not know that I saw him. He was trying to slip up behind me to scare me. I could clearly see all he was trying to do. I could see it all plainly. I knew what he was doing. So, I pretended to not see him and let him supposedly scare me. So he came up behind me and said boo to scare me. I knew exactly that he was going to do this. When he said boo, I turned around with the gun and almost pulled the trigger. I stopped just in the instant of time from killing him. It was like a spirit took over me. I know now that this was exactly what happened.

What happened in the hunting experience, also happened another time. When I was young man, in my twenties, I was living in Cleveland, Ohio of the United States. I was not married and not saved at that time. I for some reason had bought a pistol and started carrying it on me. I was with a certain woman and she said something that I did not like, I pulled out my pistol and was getting ready to pull the trigger, to kill her. I stopped just in the instant of time before I pulled the trigger. It was like my sound mind came back to me before I pulled the trigger. I said to myself, what in the world is this that I was about to do. I know now that it was God who ran those evil spirits from me. Very soon after that experience, I came from Cleveland on a vacation to Mobile, Alabama. This is where I am now writing this Book, where my family and I live. On this vacation, my cousin, that I mentioned earlier, and I were fishing. We were fishing in about the same place where I almost killed him when we were hunting. I had the pistol in my holster that I bought in Cleveland with me. We were fishing in a very shallow stream of the creek, about a foot deep. It was clear water. We could see the bottom of the creek. I leaned over to put my hook in the water and the pistol fell out of my holster into the clear water about a foot from me. My cousin and I searched the clear, shallow, water for about an hour looking for the pistol and never found it. I know now that it was God that caused me to lose that pistol/gun. I probably would have killed someone. God just had an angel to hide that pistol so we could not find it. Satan would have made me kill someone.

We know that God has a Plan for Mankind, but Satan also has a Plan for Mankind. Consider what would Satan's Plan be? What would Satan who hates Mankind Plan be? What would Satan who is jealous and envious of Mankind Plan be? Satan who is a murderer, what would his Plan for Mankind be? Well, Satan would base his Plan on efforts to combat God's Plan for Mankind. God's Plan for Mankind is to save Mankind. It is God's desire that we would all be saved.

II Peter Ch. 3, V. 9
"The Lord is not slack concerning his promise, as some men count slackness; but is longsuffering to us-ward, not willing that any should perish, but that all should come to repentance."

Every since Adam and Eve listened to the voice of Satan in the Garden of Eden and, therefore, denounced the God Almighty and were kicked out of the Garden of Eden, God has a had a Plan in the making to redeem Mankind. The Plan was fully executed when JESUS died on the cross and was buried and rose from the dead after three days and three nights. Well, Satan's Plan is that he will simply deceive Mankind not to believe what JESUS has said. Satan's main source of this deception is carried out through his preachers, such as, those two that we mentioned earlier. JESUS said, to be redeemed, to be saved, that you must be born again and then obey God's word. Born again means to be born of God. What do you imagine what Satan would be Planning to combat this. Satan would simply have his ministers to establish a lie on being born of God.

John Ch. 3, Vs. 3 & 5

"Jesus answered and said unto him, Verily, verily, I say unto thee, Except a man be born again, he cannot see the kingdom of God. Jesus answered, Verily, verily, I say unto thee, Except a man be born of water and of the Spirit, he cannot enter into the kingdom of God."

Later in this Book we provide you with four easy steps how to be born again.

Satan has known about God's Plan to redeem Mankind for many years; every since Adam and Eve's time.

Genesis Ch. 3, V. 15

"And I will put enmity between thee and the woman, and between thy seed and her seed; it shall bruise thy head, and thou shalt bruise his heel."

So, Satan has been at work every since the days of Adam and Eve to carry out his Plan for Mankind. What do you think a cunning Planner would do? He would of course try to influence how Mankind thinks. He would understand that since God mentioned that man's off spring would be against him, but some for him, then, therefore, Satan saw his opportunity. Satan saw that God was pleased with Abel and not pleased with Cain. Satan's most characteristic sins and first sins were jealousy and envy. Satan, therefore, imparted these two sins, jealousy and envy, into Cain, thereby, causing Cain to kill Abel. As time passed, Satan saw how easy it was to control Mankind. As history continued to shed time, Satan noticed that God said through Solomon, God's wises servant, that money could control all things.

<u>Ecclesiastes Ch. 10,V. 19</u>
"A feast is made for laughter, and wine maketh merry: but money answered all things."

Understanding this, Satan launched an all-out effort to get money into the hands of those who would be most useful to him. Satan surmised that if he could get money into the hands of the most ignorant and stupid of Mankind, then he would have a great advantage in this war for souls. So Satan has made sure that the most ignorant and stupid would control the riches of the world; which turned out to be Cain's off spring, pale people.

Most of the mental retarded and mentally disturbed among people is nothing more than demon/unclean spirit/ evil spirit possession. Most of this possession comes from witchcraft or sodomy/homosexuality. Most of this demon/unclean spirit/evil spirit possession is called:

1. Down Syndrome
2. Autism
3. Schizophrenia
4. Etc.

These have been the names given by the Psychiatrist. Who themselves are nothing more than witchcraft workers. God says that the demon/unclean spirit/evil spirit should be cast out of people. To do this, you must have the Spirit, the Holy Ghost. If you have God's Spirit you speak in tongues. The world's and Satan's answer to the problem of this possession is to take the counsel of a Psychiatrist. JESUS said that a devil cannot cast out a devil. Thus you have the Psychiatrist's counsel/advice.

Matthew Ch. 12, Vs. 22-28

"Then was brought unto him one possessed with a devil, blind, and dumb: and he healed him, insomuch that the blind and dumb both spake and saw. And all the people were amazed, and said, Is this the son of David? But when the Pharisees heard it, they said, This fellow doth not cast out devils, but by Beelzebub the prince of devils. And Jesus knew their thoughts, and said unto them, Every kingdom divided against itself is brought to desolation; and every city or house divided against itself shall not stand: And if Satan cast out Satan, he is divided against himself; how shall then his kingdom stand? And if Beelzebub cast out devils, by whom do your children cast them out? Therefore they shall be your judges. But I cast out devils by the Spirit of God . . ."

Most of this mental retardation or mental problems are among Cain's off spring, pale people, white folks. It is not hardly a family among them who do not have this mental retardation or mental problems. This is because it is not hardly a family among them who are not demon/ unclean spirit/evil spirit possessed. This is because it is not hardly a family among them who do not practice witchcraft and who are not homosexuals.

Consider this. Suppose that you gathered all of these demon/unclean spirit/evil spirit possessed people together and make a society of them and give them all the money to do what they want. What would you eventually get? You would get Cain's off spring, pale people, white folks. You would get such as the United States, Great Britain, Russia and the other European societies. God, himself, told and showed me back in the summer of the Year of 2000, that Former President George W. Bush was like a mentally retarded child.

You might say, I do not believe that such scheming has been done to control mankind by Satan. I say to you, yes it has been and yes it is. I have not written of this before. Not in all of our previous other (45) forty-five Books, have I written this. God took me to another planet. I was on a mission for God, but I do not know what the mission was. God put me in a large building complex on the planet. I was there spying on the occupants of the building complex. I knew, somehow through God's revelation to my mine, that if they caught me they would kill me. I would be dead. There were men there in the building complex. They were dressed in clothing of modern day suits; such as would be in a typical office job in our society here in the United States. These men, and they all were men, were constantly planning evil. Every imagination, every word and every deed of theirs were evil. As I continued to spy and observe them, I was discovered by them. They were about to catch me and kill me and just at that moment God translated me to heaven. I will not tell any more at this time. These men on this planet were Satan's helpers; fallen angels or demons, evil spirits or whatever you want to call them. They were constantly and continually planning evil. This planning of the evil spirits/fallen angels was against God and Mankind. These helpers of Satan were on another planet. I do not know what planet. Angels, including fallen angels, evil spirits, look like human beings. Remember, God said let us make man in our own image.

Genesis Ch. 1, Vs. 26 & 27

"And God said let us make man in our own image, after our likeness . . . So God created man in his own image, in the image of God created he him . . ."

Also, the Book of Hebrews of the New Testament of the Holy Scriptures/Bible indicates that fallen angels/evil spirits look like men.

Hebrews Ch. 13, V. 2
"Be not forgetful to entertain strangers: for thereby some have entertained angels unawares."

The evil spirit/fallen angel/familiar spirit is who people see when they say that they saw or spoke to a dead person who they recognized that was not saved. Let us be clear here. No one is or has been saved unless he or she spoke in tongues. You might say, I KNOW THAT MY MOTHER, FATHER, CHILD OR WHOEVER WAS SAVED and they did not speak in tongues. If you know that they were saved, then we say unto you, they spoke in tongues before they died at some point and time and you just did not know it. For those who were not saved or who are saved, neither they nor Satan nor any of his helpers, has any power to get anyone out of hell or heaven. They pretend to do so to get your money. Some have pointed to the Holy Scriptures of I Samuel Chapter 28, regarding Saul talking to the witch of Endor, to say that a witch or warlock/wizard can bring someone back from the dead. They, the witch or warlock/wizard, sadly misrepresent the Scriptures to you. You, as well as they, are ignorant of God's word. You must remember/understand at this point and time that God had rejected Saul and turned him over to lying spirits.

I Samuel Ch. 28, Vs. 7-14

"Then said Saul unto his servants, Seek me a woman that hath a familiar spirit, that I may go to her, and inquire of her. And his servant said to him, Behold, there is a woman that hath a familiar spirit at Endor. And Saul disguised himself, and put on other raiment, and he went, and two men with him, and they came to the woman by night: and he said, I pray thee, divine unto me by the familiar spirit, and bring me him up, whom I shall name unto thee. And the woman said unto him, Behold, thou knowest what Saul hath done, how he hath cut off those that have familiar spirits, and the wizards, out of the land: where then layest thou a snare for my life, to caused me to die? And Saul sware to her by the LORD, saying, As the LORD liveth, there shall no punishment happen to thee for this thing. Then said the woman, Whom shall I bring up unto thee? And he said, Bring me up Samuel. And when the woman saw Samuel, she cried with a loud voice: and the woman spake to Saul, saying, Why hath thou deceived me? for thou art Saul. And the king said unto her, Be not afraid: for what sawest thou? And the woman said unto Saul, I saw gods ascending out of the earth. And he said unto her, What form is he of? And she said, An old man cometh up; and he is covered with a mantle. And Saul perceived that it was Samuel, and he stooped with his face to the ground, and bowed himself."

The above Scriptures are what the witches and wizards/ warlocks use to trick the people that they are calling up someone from the dead. The "familiar spirit" tag is so-called because the demon/evil spirit/familiar spirit is pretending to be the person supposedly called up from the dead. The spirit is imitating the dead person. These witches and wizards/warlocks know it. THEY TRICK YOU TO GET YOUR MONEY. God had Samuel to appear before the witch could even start practicing her witchcraft. Look again at those Scriptures. It was said, "Then said the woman, Whom shall I bring up unto thee? And he said, bring me up Samuel. And when the woman saw Samuel, she cried with a loud voice." The witch was surprised. Why was she surprised? She was use to the demon/evil spirit/familiar spirit pretending to be the person. The woman was surprised because God had Samuel to appear. God did it. God did it before the witch and the familiar spirit could begin there deceit.

Many people practice witchcraft and do not know it. They do not understand that when they go to those witches, wizards/warlocks, palm readers, psychics, magicians and the likes, they are practicing witchcraft.

It is almost a guarantee, that when you go from God, you go into witchcraft. This includes people who God has withdrawn his Spirit from. So, when Cain went out from the presence of God, he went into witchcraft.

Genesis Ch. 4, V. 16
"And Cain went out from the presence of the LORD, and dwelt in the land of Nod, on the east of Eden."

Let us give you this further counsel concerning something that we said earlier. We mentioned that God translated me to another planet where there were evil spirits there planning evil. There are not any other human beings on other planets. However, this experience of God taking me to another planet where there were evil spirits on it, let me know that there might be other of God's creation, other than human beings, that could be on other planets. For all of you who somehow think that you can go to another planet to escape God's judgment, you are mistaken.

Acts Ch. 17, Vs. 24 & 26
"God . . . hath made of one blood all nations of men for to dwell on all the face of the earth, and hath determined the times before appointed, and the bounds of their habitation . . ."

The idea of other human beings living on other planets is a lie from Satan. Satan perverts God's word in the Holy Scriptures of Ezekiel Chapter 1 of the Old Testament.

Ezekiel Ch. 1, Vs. 4-28 & Ch. 3, Vs. 12-14
"And I looked, and behold, a whirlwind came out of the north, a great cloud, and a fire infolding itself, and

a brightness was about it, and out of the midst thereof as the colour of amber, out of the midst of the fire. Also out of the midst thereof came the likeness of four living creatures. And this was there appearance; they had the likeness of a man. And every one had four faces, and every one had four wings. And their feet were straight feet; and the sole of their feet was like the sole of a calf's foot: and they sparkled as the colour of burnished brass. And they had the hands of a man under their wings on their four sides; and they four had their faces and their wings. Their wings were joined one to another; they turned not when they went; they went every one straight forward. As for the likeness of their faces, they four had the face of a man, and the face of a lion, on the right side: and they four had the face of an ox on the left side; they four also had the face of an eagle. Thus were their faces: and their wings were stretched upward; two wings of every one were joined one to another, and two covered their bodies. And they went every one straight forward: whither the spirit was to go, they went; and they turned not when they went. As for the likeness of the living creatures, their appearance was like burning coals of fire, and like the appearance of lamps: it went up and down among the living creatures; and the fire was bright, and out of the fire went forth lightning. And the living creatures ran and returned as the appearance of a flash of lightning. Now as I beheld the living creatures, behold one wheel upon the earth by the living creatures, with his four faces. The appearance of the wheels and their work was like unto the colour of a beryl: and they four had one likeness: and their appearance and their work was as it were a wheel in the middle of a wheel. When they went, they went upon their four sides: and they turned not when they went. As for their rings, they were so high that they were dreadful; and their rings were full of eyes round about them four. And when the living creatures went, the wheels went by them: and when the living creatures were lifted up from the earth, the wheels were lifted up. Whithersoever the spirit was to go, they went, thither was their spirit to go; and the wheels were lifted up over against them: for the spirit of the living creature was in the wheels. When those went, these went; and when those stood, these stood; and when those were lifted up from the earth, the wheels were lifted up over against them: for the spirit of the living creature was in the wheels. And the likeness of the firmament upon the heads of the living creature was as the colour of the terrible crystal, stretched forth over their heads above. And under the firmament were their wings straight, the one toward the other: every one had two, which covered on this side, and every one had two, which covered on that side, their bodies. And when they went, I heard the noise of their wings, like the noise of great waters, as the voice of the Almighty, the voice of speech, as the noise of an host: when they stood, they let down their wings. And there was a voice from the firmament that was over their heads, when they stood, and had let down their wings. And above the firmament

even lying to the Almighty God. Yes, you might say, you have shown that white people have a tendency toward taking what is not their own. Yes, you might say, you have shown that white people have a strong tendency to steal. Yes, you might say, you have shown that the God Almighty has said some very critical and demeaning things about white people. Yes, you might say, you have revealed that the Almighty God has said that no white people were saved in Biblical times. Yes, you might say, you have pointed out that very few of the white people will be in the first resurrection, the so-called rapture. Yes, you might say, you have shown that white people have mastered the practice of witchcraft and have prospered because it. Yes, you might say, Yes, Yes, Yes, you have shown, you have revealed, you have pointed out, but what is the value of it all. Why write the Book? First of all, we write the Book because God Almighty told us to. Secondly, we write the Book to fulfill the Scriptures written by Apostle John and Apostle Matthew of the New Testament of the Holy Scriptures/Bible.

John Ch. 8, V. 32
"And ye shall know the truth and the truth shall make you free."

Matthew Ch. 10, V. 26
". . . for there is nothing covered that shall not be revealed: and hid that shall not be known."

You might ask, why would God want to make it known? Well, God in his wisdom to make it known, frees the world of the witchcraft over all of non-white mankind. White people through its witchcraft have made all the world to desire to be like them; to be like them even in the curse of their skin color. Yes, they have made a curse from God in the frailness of their skin color to be something to be desired. How great has been their witchcraft. Very few on this earth have not wanted the paleness of skin like white folks. The slaves taken from Africa by white folks, pale people, to the Americas, were made, through the mind control witchcraft, to strive to get rid of all the Blackness of their skin that was possible. This mind control witchcraft was carried out through a process called natural selection. All would seek and strive to get rid of the Blackness of their skin through breeding of having children with a white person, pale person or lighter complexion person.

For those who achieved/accomplished to become of a lighter complexion, they were rewarded by allowing them a better status in their captivity or oppression. In the case of slavery in the United States, the slaves were allowed to serve their so-called masters in his house. Other forms of this reward system was carried out also through other means. Always, however, the lighter your complexion, the better it was for you. This selection, this discrimination, eventually had the desired effect that the slave master wanted. The Black people wanted to look white/pale. This in turn would cause them not to or diminish the captives rising up against the slave master because they wanted to be like him. The mind control witchcraft would have had its desired effect. Refer to our Book, "God Said Black People In The United States Are Jews". Also, refer to an expected upcoming Book with the Title "I Use To Be An Uncle Tom". We will not reveal the Author's name at this time. All of the above of this mind control witchcraft was what God was indicating would happen from the very beginning in Genesis Chapter 4.

Genesis Ch. 4, Vs. 6 & 7
"And the LORD said unto Cain, Why art thou wroth? And why art thou contenance fallen? And if thou doest well, shalt thou not be accepted? And if thou doest not well, sin lieth at the door. And unto thee shall be his desire, and thou shall rule over him."

The United States, Cuba, Mexico, Dominican Republic, Brazil, Columbia, Chilli, Venezuela, Haiti, Guatemala, Virgin Island, Bahamas and others of the Americas, were all witchcraft to rid themselves of the Blackness of their skin. Satan and white people made a curse from God to be something that is desired. Incredible! Absolutely Incredible!

Not only did Black and non-Black Jews strive to look white/pale, but others of the world also obsession was to be more white/pale looking. Yes, God told us from the very beginning that it would happen. The reason it has taken so long to understand this mind control witchcraft, lies also in the Holy Scriptures.

Matthew Ch. 10, V. 26
". . . for there is nothing covered that shall not be revealed; and hid that shall not be known."

Genesis Ch. 4, V. 7
". . . And unto thee shall be his desire, an thou shall rule over him."

Daniel Ch. 12, Vs. 8 & 9
"And I heard, but I understood not: then said I, O my lord, what shall be the ends of these things? And he said, Go thy way, Daniel: for the words are closed up and sealed to the time of the end."

The reason it has taken so long for this mind control witchcraft to be broken is because of God's people, the Jews, Black and non-Black, continual disobedience to God's word. God saw from the very beginning to the end what his people would do and, therefore, God could say the words that he said. God used Satan, through Cain's off spring, pale people, white people, to have most of his people to desire a curse and to have Cain's off spring, white people, pale people, to rule over them because of their disobedience. Not all of God's people disobeyed him, but most of them did.

Skin color and associated facial features were not the only things that the world and even some of God's people tried to imitate of white people, pale people. They also tried to imitate their life style and culture. Satan smiled. Satan's Plan for Mankind was really taking shape. This is why that you see the whole world taking on the culture of Cain's off spring, white folks, pale people. Refer to our Books:

1. "The Whole World Becoming As Sodom"
2. "Words From God, By God Appearing To Us Or Just Talking To Us, For The End Times"
3. "March Was When JESUS Was Born And Not Christmas"
4. "God Said Black People In The United States Are Jews"

Remember this, as we mentioned earlier, one of the names that represent the United States that is in the Holy Scriptures of the New Testament is Sodom. So, Cain's off spring, pale people, white people, are also known for sodomy/homosexuality. This is the life style that the whole world is trying to imitate. Refer to our Books:

1. "The Whole World Becoming As Sodom"

2. "Words From God, By God Appearing To Us Or Just Talking To Us, For The End Times"
3. "March Was When JESUS Was Born And Not Christmas"

<u>Revelation Ch. 11, Vs. 3,7 & 8</u>
"And I will give power unto my two witnesses . . . And when they shall have finished their testimony, the beast . . . shall overcome them, and kill them. And their dead bodies shall lie in the street of the great city, which spiritually is called Sodom . . ."

God warned his people in the Holy Scriptures/Bible not to imitate the heathen.

<u>Jeremiah Ch. 10, Vs. 1 & 2</u>
"Hear ye the word which the LORD speaketh unto you, O house of Israel: Thus saith the LORD, Learn not the way of the heathen . . ."

<u>I Kings Ch. 14, V. 24</u>
"And there were also sodomites in the land: and they did according to all the abominations of the nations which the LORD cast out before the children of Israel."

Now you know, one of the main reasons why God had Israel to kill the people in Biblical days/times; it was because they were sodomites/homosexuals. This is also one of the reasons why God will have the United States destroyed.

Starting with Former President Bill Clinton's Administration, the United States passed a law, that if you speak certain things against a homosexual/ sodomite, it would be a crime. The elevation of them, the homosexuals/sodomites, were carried to a higher level during Former President George W. Bush's Administration; even though during his Administration his Party, the Republicans, had control over everything; the Presidency, the House of Representatives, the Senate and Supreme Court. Yet, laws were passed in certain States giving civil liberties to sodomites/homosexuals and their partners. The height of immorality, sin, reached its despicable and repugnant low under President Barack Obama's Presidency. Well, during President Barack Obama's Administration, homosexuals/sodomites reached one of their main goals. A president, President Barack Obama, declared that it should be the law of the land that homosexuals/sodomites should be given the official seal of approval by the Government to marry in all of the states of the United States. The United States' Supreme Court recently, during the writing of this Book, ruled on a case that essentially gave the stamp of approval by the United States officially recognizing sodomites/homosexuals to marry.

Although the last three Presidents have overtly done things to promote homosexuality/sodomy, as we have written before, all of the Presidents from George Washington to Barack Obama have been sodomites. Refer to our Books:

1. "The Whole World Becoming As Sodom"
2. "Words From God, By God Appearing To Us Or Just Talking To Us, For The End Times"
3. "The Judgment Of The United States"

In this day and time we would call the First President of the United States, George Washington, and those of that day, transvestites. A transvestite is a man who dresses up as a woman and a woman who dresses up as a man. George Washington and the other men of that day wore wigs. They also wore panty hoses. They also wore ruffles on their shirts as women wore and do wear. The men also shaved their face to be naked as a woman.

All of the immediate above paragraphs, just validates the word God; a word spoken by God (2,000) two thousand years ago. The United States is the modern day Sodom.

Also, the United States destiny with sodomy/ homosexuality is revealed by taking a close look at Egypt of old as being the spiritual equivalent of the United States. Sodomy/homosexuality was so prevalent in Egypt of old, until marriage between man and woman was such a rarity, until the reproduction of Egyptians was so low, that the children of Israel out-numbered them. Only (70) seventy of the children of Israel came to out-number the whole of Egypt.

Exodus Ch. 1, Vs. 7-9
"And the children of Israel were fruitful, and increased abundantly, and multiplied, and waxed exceeding mighty; and the land was filled with them. Now there arose up a new king over Egypt, which knew not Joseph. And he said unto his people, Behold, the people of the children of Israel are more and mightier than we . . ."

Why did sodomites/homosexuals become hypocrites? Why did they want to hide being a sodomite/ homosexual? This is a result of one main thing. This is a result of sodomites/homosexuals taking on the title of Christians. This happened with the emergence of the man in Rome winning the power struggle to be over the Church when Apostle John died. This emergence of control over, the then perverted Church by the man in Rome, he to eventually be called the Pope, made it impossible to be known as a sodomite at the same time calling yourself a Christian. Thus, the deceit was born. Thus, being a hypocrite of who you are was born. It was just too much written in the word of God against being a sodomite to hide or overlook.

Genesis Ch. 18, V. 20
"And the LORD said, Because the cry of Sodom and Gomorrah is great, and because their sin is very grievous . . ."

Genesis Ch. 19, Vs. 1,12 & 13
"And their came two angels to Sodom . . . And the men said unto Lot . . . we will destroy this place, because the cry of them is waxen great before the face of the LORD; and the LORD hath sent us to destroy it."

Leviticus Ch. 18, V. 22
"Thou shalt not lie with mankind, as with womankind: it is abomination."

Leviticus Ch. 18, V. 27
"(For all these abominations . . . the land is defiled:)"

Romans Ch. 1, Vs. 24-29 & 32
"Wherefore God also gave them up to uncleanness through the lusts of their own hearts . . . Who changed the truth of God into a lie . . . For this cause God gave them up into vile affections: for even their women did change the natural use into that which is against nature: And likewise also the men, leaving the natural use of the woman, burned in their lust one toward another; men with men working that which is unseemly, and receiving in themselves that recompense of their error was meet. And even as they did not like to retain God

APOSTLE Frederick E. Franklin

in their knowledge, God gave them up to a reprobate mind . . . Being filled with all unrighteousness . . . Who knowing the judgment of God, that they which commit such things are worthy of death, not only do the same, but have pleasure in them that do them."

This so-called Christian identity of the sodomites/ homosexuals had to happen because the (Anti-Christ) Beast had to come forth in the end times from the so-called Christians. The Former Pope, Pope John Paul II, Carol Josef Wojtyla, will be the so-called (Anti-Christ) Beast.

The off spring of Cain, white folks, pale people, have perfected lying. They have trained their society to lie by what they call acting. They even reward the best liar with a golden stature called the Oscar.

John Ch. 8, V. 44
"Ye are of your father the devil, and the lusts of your father ye will do. He was a murderer from the beginning, and abode not in the truth, because there is no truh in him. When he speaketh a lie, he speaketh of his own: for he is a liar, and the father of it."

Think about this, Cain's off spring, pale people, white folks, reward the best liar/actor/actress with a golden stature called the Oscar. What makes this any different than idol god worshippers of old? They are no different than those mentioned in the Holy Scriptures/Bible and that which was written about the pagans.

There are some good white folks. There are some of the off spring of Cain, pale people, white folks, who are good. Likewise, there are some who are not Cain's off spring who are bad. You might from all that has been written thus far, ask how could this be? You might wonder, how could there be any good white folks? It can be so, because God is in control.

Proverbs Ch. 21, V. 1
"THE king's heart is in the hand of the LORD, as the rivers of water: he turneth it withersoever he will."

Psalm 24, V. 1
"The earth is the LORD's, and the fullness thereof; the world, and they that dwell therein."

An example of God turning the king's heart for what God wanted him to do, can be seen when God caused the Pharaoh to promote Joseph, a slave, to be over all of Egypt. The Pharaoh made Joseph to be second in power to himself.

Genesis Ch. 37, V. 28
". . . and they drew and lift up Joseph out of the pit, and sold Joseph to the Ishmeelites for twenty pieces of silver: and they brought Joseph into Egypt."

Genesis Ch. 41, V. 39-44

"And Pharaoh said unto Joseph, Forasmuch as God hath shewed thee all this, there is none so discreet and wise as thou art: Thou shalt be over my house, and according unto thy word shall all my people be ruled: only in the throne will I be greater than thou. And Pharaoh said unto Joseph, See, I have set the over all the land of Egypt. And Pharaoh took off his ring from his hand, and put it upon Joseph's hand, and arrayed him in vestures of fine linen, and put a golden chain about his neck; And he made him to ride in the second chariot which he had: and they cried before him, Bow the knee: and he made him ruler over all the land of Egypt. And Pharaoh said unto Joseph, I am Pharaoh, and without thee shall no man lift up his hand or foot in all the land of Egypt."

Yes, you might say, but that was in Biblical days. You might say, God does not do any like that now. Well, consider this. President Barack Obama an off spring of slaves of the United States, defeated a white man for the Presidency who is one of the riches men in the world, the riches ever to run for the Presidency. President Barack Obama defeated Mitt Romney. This only could have happen if the controversial "Obama Care" was ruled to be legal by the United States' Supreme Court. The United States' Supreme Court is and was control during the Presidential Election by Mitt Romney's main Republican supporters. The Justices of the Supreme

Court was evenly split and only the Chief Justice could break the tie; Chief Justice John Roberts. Chief Justice John Roberts is and was during the Presidential Election a great enemy/opponent of President Barack Obama. His bitterness toward President Barack Obama was and is so great that he fumble an age old custom and duty of the Chief Justice of swearing in Barack Obama to be President during his first term in office. Now for the second term to determine the Presidency; here comes the Chief Justice's vote on "Obama Care", with the whole world watching, and Mitt Romney and the Republicans already celebrating. Chief Justice John Roberts voted for "Obama Care", thereby, delivering the Presidency to Barack Obama.

I know that Chief Justice John Roberts is having many sleepless nights wondering why he voted that way. Let us give you some rest. The king's heart as well as the Chief Justice heart are in the hand of the LORD, as the rivers of water, HE turneth it withersoever HE will.

The Chief Justice, John Roberts, was so mad, so disgusted, so outraged, with his vote on "Obama Care" which delivered the Presidential Election to President Barack Obama, that he gutted the Voting Rights Act which helped Black people. Little does he know, God will also use this to help Black people.

So, we see no matter what Satan has planned for Cain's off spring, pale people, white folks, God can still/yet do what he wants. God said he will have mercy on whoever he desires.

Romans Ch. 9, V. 15
"For he saith to Moses, I will have mercy on whom I will have mercy, and I will have compassion on whom I will have compassion."

There are some good white folks. God let us know that there are even some white folks that will be saved. Although very few of the very few, some will be saved. Some will be in the First Resurrection, the so-called rapture. God even prophesied through my wife, Prophetess Sylvia Franklin, some years ago, that there will be some white folks under my Apostleship. God showed that one of them will be a very famous woman who is known throughout the earth. God showed me, also some years ago, that I will be laying hands on people anointing them with gifts to go and minister. Among them were a few white people.

Let us say this. Not all at this point in time of Cain's off spring are sodomites/homosexuals. There are a few who are not. Refer to our Books:

1.   "The Whole World Becoming As Sodom"

2.   "Words From God, By God Appearing To Us
      Or Just Talking To Us, For The End Times"

Let us say a few words about this. It has been said by
most of sodomites/homosexuals that they were born
that way. The life style of those involved in sodomy/
homosexuality is a sin. All sin is from Satan. The person
who chooses this life style chooses to sin. Those who
are sodomites/homosexuals have been possessed by
Satan or demons/evil spirits. If sodomites/homosexuals
have children their babies and children are possessed
by Satan or demons/evil spirits. So, it goes on and on,
generation after generation. There is one way for this
chain to be broken. The sodomite/homosexual MUST
be born again. The person MUST be filled with Holy
Ghost/Spirit and get baptized in the name of JESUS.
When you are filled with the Holy Ghost/Spirit you
speak in tongues as the Spirit gives the utterance. When
you are baptized you MUST be baptized in the name
of JESUS. Both are essential to be delivered from this
sodomy/homosexuality and to stay delivered. Later on
in this Book we provide four easy steps on how to get
delivered and to stay delivered; to be born again. Refer
to our Books:

1.   "The Whole World Becoming As Sodom"
2.   "Words From God, By God Appearing To Us
      Or Just Talking To Us, For The End Times"

Not only is the above, the only way for Cain's off spring to be delivered from sodomy/homosexuality, but also all others; Black people and all non-Cain's off spring.

Although a sodomite/homosexual is an abomination to God, there is, however, someone who is worse than that in God's eye sight. The worst to God that is on this earth is in great abundance. The worst, even worse than a sodomite/homosexual, is one who rejects God's word. Look at what God said in the Holy Scriptures/Bible in the New Testament. Refer to Matthew Chapter 10, Verse 14 & 15.

<u>Matthew Ch. 10, Vs. 14 & 15</u>
"And whosoever shall not receive you, nor hear your words, when ye depart out of that house or city, shake off the dust off your feet. Verily I say unto you, It shall be more tolerable for the land of Sodom and Gomorarrha in the day of judgment, than for that city."

Consider this however. What would be God's view of a sodomite/homosexual who rejects God's word.

It seems like whatever God said not to do, Satan has caused man to do it. It seems like whatever God has said that is filthy and not to touch, Satan has had man to touch. It seems like whatever God has told man not to do, Satan has man doing it. Whatever God has said in his word, the Scriptures, Satan has perverted through his children, including Cain's off spring.

God loves all of his natural creation, but God expects his particular creation to function as God intended. For instance, God told man to dominate his other natural creation on earth. God did not expect a worm or cat or dog or bird or lizard, etc., to rule over man.

Genesis Ch. 1, Vs. 26-28
"And God said, Let us make man in our image, after our likeness: and let them have dominion over the fish of the sea, and over the fowl of the air, and over the cattle, and over all the earth, and over every creeping thing that creepeth upon the earth. So God created man in his own image, in the image of God created him; male and female created he them. And God bless them, and said unto them, Be fruitful, and multiply, and replenish the earth and subdue it: and have dominion over the fish of the sea, and over the fowl of the air, and over every living thing that moveth upon the earth."

So, God expects none of his other natural creation on earth to be like man. God never expects a dog, cat or whatever to be like man. A dog has his place; a cat has his place; a bird has his place; etc. has his place. Satan, however, has man having so-called pets; even pets that live in man's house; even pets that sleep in his/her bed; even pets that man has sex with. Having pets such as dogs and cats in the house is animal abuse. Those who do these things say that they are showing love for animals, but actually it is the opposite. God made a dog to roam free. God made a cat to roam free. God made a dog and a cat to be free to hunt for their food. To be free to choose a mate. To be free to give birth. To be free to fight or to run. All of these things makes the dog and cat whole; what they are supposed to be. Man with his fake love, has, however, imprisoned the dog and cat. Man has robbed the beast from the dog and cat. Man has even rendered much of the species of the dog and cat of the ability to reproduce. Man call it spading and neutering. What cruelty! What Selfishness! For your pleasure, you rod another of its pleasure. The pleasure of the beast to roam free and reproduce. Then, you, man, hypocritically, say that you love animals. Then after all of this, you then pervert the dog and cat by having sex with them. Cain! Cain! Cain!

In the case of a dog, God has indicated that a dog is a filthy beast. A beast that should be undesirable for habitation with man.

Exodus Ch. 11, V. 7
"But against any of the children of Israel shall not a dog move his tongue, against man or beast: that ye may know that the LORD doth put a difference between the Egyptians and Israel."

Deuteronomy Ch. 23, V. 18

"Thou shalt not bring the hire of a whore, or the price of a dog, into the house of the LORD thy God for any vow: for even both these are abomination unto the LORD thy God."

Proverbs Ch. 26, V. 11

"As a dog returneth to his vomit, so a fool returneth to his folly."

Luke Ch. 16, Vs. 19-20

"There was a certain rich man, which was clothed in purple and fine linen, and fared sumptuously every day: and there was a certain beggar named Lazarus, which was laid at his gate, full of sores, And desiring to be fed with the crumbs which fell from the rich man's table: moreover the dogs came and licked his sores."

Revelation Ch. 22, Vs. 14 & 15

"Blessed are they that do his commandment, that they may have right to the tree of life, and may enter in through the gates into the city. For without are dogs, and sorceries, and whoremongers, and murderers, and idolaters, and whosoever loveth and maketh a lie."

Whether God is referring to the dog himself or referring to a man as a dog, it is a demeaning statement. How many of white folks, pale people, Cain's off spring, have dogs and cats in their house? How many of white folks, pale people, Cain's off spring, have dogs and cats in their bed? How many of white folks, pale people, Cain's off spring, have dogs and cats licking their face and mouth?

Cain's off spring, white folks, pale people, also have some of the rest of Mankind imitating them regarding dogs and cats. After learning these things which we have written what God says about dogs and cats, will Cain's off spring, white folks, pale people, repent of their filthy ways? We think not. Now you can understand, even another reason why so very few of Cain's off spring, white folks, pale people, will be saved; will be in the First Resurrection, the so-called rapture.

The filthy part, sex with animals, of Cain's off spring's, white folk's, pale people, culture is beastality. Not all have drop to this low, but nearly all are headed this way. Beastality is a man or woman having sex with an animal. The obsession of Cain's off spring, white folks, pale people, having pets living in their house is the path to this abomination. Satan will cause it to happen. Satan is filthy. During these last days, the end times, will be a time on the earth when all sins that ever was will be manifested. Beastality was done in days of old and is/ will be done in this day.

Exodus Ch. 22, V. 19

"Whosoever lieth with a beast shall surely be put to death."

Leviticus Ch. 18, V. 23

"Neither shalt thou lie with any beast to defile thyself therewith: neither shall any woman stand before a beast to lie down thereto: it is confusion."

Leviticus Ch. 20, Vs. 15 & 16

"And if any man lie with a beast, he shall surely be put to death: and ye shall slay the beast. And if any woman approach unto any beast, and lie down thereto, thou shall kill the woman and the beast: they shall surely be put to death; their blood shall be upon them."

Deuteronomy Ch. 27, V. 21

"Cursed be he that lieth with any manner of beast . . ."

Let us be clear. We and you should not kill people in this day and time. We are under a New Covenant with God. If there is any killing done for unrighteousness, God himself will do it. It is even against the law to kill an animal in the United States. This law was passed during Former President George W. Bush's time in office.

If beastality was not being done, then God would not have had so much to say about it. As the end of time approaches, immorality and sin are increasing.

When I was a sinner, in my middle to latter (20's) twenties, while living in Cleveland, Ohio of the United States, I often went to bars or night clubs. One evening as I entered a bar, a porno movie was being showed in there. I, a seasoned sinner, was shocked. I had never seen such before. White folks, pale people, men and women, were having sex with animals. It almost made me vomit. They were having sex with cows, horses, dogs, goats, hogs, chickens and maybe some other animals; including oral sex; the people performing oral sex on the animals. These were people who looked like anybody you might see on the job, in the store or church. After viewing this pornography, I was never the same again. I was a whoremonger, but I could not have sex for about two weeks. Every time I would see a white person, I would think of them having sex with an animal. Every time I would see a white person with a pet, I thought of them having sex with the animal. The above happened in the early (70's) seventies. That was about (40) forty years ago. How much more is the abomination now.

The Almighty God is a good God. The Almighty God is the good God. In spite of being the off spring of Cain and all that this implies, God will yet allow a few of the enemies of his people to be saved. If they repent of their evil, they yet can be saved like all others who will be saved. All MUST repent and get born again and obey God's word. All MUST speak in tongues as God give the utterance and get baptized in the name of JESUS for the remission of their sins and obey God's word to be saved. Refer to our Book "The Door Is Closing On The Last Opportunity For Immortality".

Not many white people, Cain's off spring, pale people, will be saved. Will you be among the few who will be saved? Or will you lie to yourself as normally has been the case as Cain's off spring, pale people, white folks, and go to hell and burn in the lake of fire.

Let us be clear. For those of us who do not have Cain's mark, non-white people, we also MUST be born again and obeys God's words to be saved; to be in the First Resurrection, the so-called rapture.

Yes, the Almighty God, the Creator of the Universe, is a good God; the good God. God is the merciful God. However, make no mistake, God will avenge his people; just like in days of old; eventually it will happen. Since the world is coming to an end, this eventuality is soon to happen. Yes, there is the judgment of the very few of the very few of the off spring of Cain being in the First Resurrection, the so-called rapture, but, also, there is a natural judgment that must take place. It will happen soon. So says God.

You might wonder/ask, if God punished his people for disobedience by having Cain's off spring, white people,

APOSTLE Frederick E. Franklin

pale people, to rule over them, then why would Cain's off spring, pale people, white folks, be judged by God? The answer to this is in the Scriptures. God said what you sow, you reap. God also indicated that he might use you to do evil, but you will have pay for that evil.

Galatians Ch. 6, V. 7
"Be not deceived; God is not mocked: for whatsoever a man soweth, that shall he also reap."

Matthew Ch. 18, V. 7
"Woe unto the world because of offenses: for it must needs be that offenses come; but woe to that man by whom the offense come."

Judas Iscariot committed an offense against JESUS. JESUS chose him to do it, but Judas had to pay for the offense of betraying JESUS. It was even prophesied many hundreds of years before it happened that Judas would have to pay for his betrayer.

Psalm 109, Vs. 6-8
". . . let Satan stand at his right hand. When he shall be judged, let him be condemned: and let his prayer become sin. Let his days be few; and let another take his office."

<u>Acts Ch. 1, Vs. 16-20</u>

"Men and brethren, this scripture must needs have been fulfilled, which the Holy Ghost by the mouth of David spake before concerning Judas, which was guide to them which took Jesus. For he was numbered with us, and had obtained part of this ministry. Now this man purchased a field with the reward of iniquity, and falling headlong, he burst asunder in the midst, and all his bowels gushed out. And it was known unto all the dwellers at Jerusalem; insomuch as that field is called in their proper tongue, Aceldama, that is to say, The field of blood. For it is written in the book of Psalm, Let his habitation be desolate, and let no man dwell therein: and his bishoprick let another take."

You must know, when it comes to his people, God will avenge them. Even though God prophesied to Abraham that Israel would go into captivity in Egypt for (400) four hundred years, God yet punished Egypt for the offense."

The main purpose of this Book is to break the power of witchcraft of Cain's off spring, white folks, pale people, off of the rest of this world. Witchcraft's power is in deceit. This Book sets the world free of the deceit that Cain's off spring, white folks, pale people, are something special or superiority and therefore, should be imitated. A deficiency/frailness/curse is not a characteristic of superior. We have given you the truth regarding Cain' off spring, white people, pale people. What the world has been bewitched to believe is a shameful deceit. A perversion of the truth is what the world has been bewitched with.

John Ch. 8, V. 32
"And ye shall know the truth, and the truth shall make you free."

We end these writings regarding Cain's Mark with this. Cain's mark will eventually lead to the 666 Mark of the (Anti-Christ) Beast. The 666 Mark of the (Anti-Christ) Beast will be based on money and who is in control. Pope John Paul II, Carol Josef Wojtyla, will be the (Anti-Christ) Beast. That old devil is not dead. He is alive and in living in the Vatican. God himself has told and shown us this. Former President Bill Clinton will administer evil on behalf of the (Anti-Christ) Beast. Former President Bill Clinton is the other beast, the False Prophet. God himself has told and shown us this. Refer to our Books:

1. "The Name Of The (Anti-Christ) Beast And 666 Identification"
2. "Who Is The False Prophet"

The wisdom of God, how great it is. God needed Cain and his off spring, white folks, pale people, to complete his Plan for the redemption of Mankind. God used

Satan to complete his Plan for Mankind. Again, even again, God made a fool out of Satan. Even again, Satan thinking himself to be slick, God makes a fool out of him. God makes a fool out of Satan to make sure that his', God's, Plan for Mankind is perfected.

Satan is nothing. Allow me this time of delight and to mock Satan. We have written of this in our Book "God Tells How To Eliminate Famine", but allow this pleasure/enjoyment again for me. [In the beginning of the Year we called 2012, GOD showed me how Satan looks and of his limits. GOD had shown me Satan (3) three or (4) four times in the past, but it was a silhouette form of Satan. In the beginning of the Year we called 2012, GOD allowed me to see in detail how Satan looks. GOD was walking with me, I believe it was GOD, it might have been an angel. We were walking toward the east. We walked up to a wall. A brick wall about (4) four feet high. The wall was at the top of an inclining area of a far distance. GOD let me know that this was Satan's territory. All of a sudden Satan came running up the incline toward us. He was loudly saying that we had no business there. At that moment a hatred came upon me against Satan like I had never experienced before. I then jumped over the wall where Satan was and began to beat him. I choked him. I beat him in his face. I kicked him. I stomped him. I squeezed him. I slapped him. I did these things over and over again. Satan was not able to do anything to me. I finally realized that I could not kill him. I then left him along and got back on the other side of the wall. He was laying down there like a whipped dog. I can tell you exactly how he looked. He was about (6) six feet to (6) six feet and (2) inches tall. He was not overweight and he was not skinny. He looked the age of a man in his forties or fifties. He looked like a white man with a tan. The shape of his head reminds you of Mitt Romney. GOD showed me this to let me know that Satan is nothing! Satan is nothing to be feared! GOD let me to beat the " snot " out of Satan to show me this. Satan has deceived some of mankind to build him up before human beings so that we as human beings will think that he is something to be feared! He is nothing! Satan is nothing! GOD, also, showed me this about Satan, to let me know that I had the victory over Satan. Some of mankind through its witchcraft/magic, divination, sorcery, make Satan look like he is something. Satan through his wizards/warlocks, witches and witchcraft workers make Satan look like he is something.

CHAPTER 2

<u>God Said Black In The United States Are Jews.</u>

(THE FINAL EXODUS)

This Chapter is an edited edition/rendering of our Book "God Said Black People In The United States Are Jews" The editing in no way changes any content of that Book. The editing was only done to adapt that Book for this Chapter and this Book.

God has said in his written word of the Holy Scriptures/ Bible that a lie cannot remain. It will eventually be made known as a lie.

<u>Matthew Ch. 10, V. 26</u>
". . . for there is nothing covered, that shall not be revealed; and hid, that shall not known."

This is the time of revealing. This is the time of unmasking. Time is running out and God cannot lie. The words of God must be fulfilled.

God said that Black People in the United States are Jews. How can this be? To answer this question we must <u>revisit</u> the past.

In the not so distant past, around the last half of 1986 or 1987, God indicated to me, a Black man in the United States, that I was a Jew, but I did not understand what God was showing me. I will get back to this later on in this book.

God said about his people in the Holy Scriptures that if they would obey him that he would bless them. God, also, in his sanctified word, said that if his people, the Jews, disobey him, that he would curse them; cursed even to the point of letting their enemies enslave them.

<u>Deuteronomy Ch. 28, Vs. 36,41 & 64-66</u>
"The LORD shall bring thee, and thy king which thou shalt set over thee, unto a nation which neither thou nor thy fathers have known; and there shalt thou serve other gods, wood and stone. Thou shalt beget sons and daughters, but thou shalt not enjoy them; for they shall go into captivity. And the LORD shall scatter thee among all the people, from the one end of the earth even unto the other . . . And among these nations shalt thou find no ease, neither shall the sole of thy foot have rest . . . And thy life shall hang in doubt before thee . . ."

You might say, this only points to the captivity of the Jews, God's people, in Egypt, Babylon and those of Adolph Hitler's captivity of Nazi Germany. I say unto you, this is partially true, but it also includes the Black

Slaves from Africa brought to the United States and their offspring.

Black People brought to the United States were brained washed by mind control witchcraft to think four main things to keep them in control:

1. that they/we were or are illiterate;
2. that they/we had no important heritage;
3. that they/we were or are inferior to white people;
4. that they/we were or are in the minority.

These four would allow the slave owners to keep the slaves under control. We will show that all four were lies and are lies.

We will first reveal this very important fact about the white slave owners and the Ku Klux Klan. God said that they were and are witchcraft workers. He, further, said that they used this witchcraft to control the slaves and the Black People of the United States. God said that the validity of these assertions is indicated in the fact that the title of the leader of the Ku Klux Klan is called the Grand Wizard. For those of you who might not know, a wizard is a warlock, a male witchcraft worker. For, further, understanding concerning this matter, refer to our Book "Words From God, By God Appearing To Us

Or Just Talking To Us, For The End Times", numbers "443" through "455".

When the slaves were shipped from Africa, they were stripped of their tribal language. The wives were separated from their husbands. The children were separated from their parents. The different tribes were mixed together so that they could not communicate. As time passed, as the elders died or were killed, there left a people with no language, and no connection to its past. This all was the scheme of the slave owners to control the slaves. The slaves were denied any means to organize or to learn a language. The slave owners would breed the women like some cattle to increase their profit. Then they would separate the children from their mothers. Even sending the children where they might never see their parents again. The only language then that the slaves would know, was the language of command from their slave owners. It is absolutely amazing what the Black People were able to accomplish. It is astonishing. It is miraculous. It had to be God with us. They/We had to have a special connection with God. They/We had to be God's special people. They/We had to be God's special people. They/We had to be Jews, <u>but how?</u>

God spoke to my wife, Prophetess Sylvia Franklin, and said, that Black People in the United States do not know who we are. God said that this is the reason we cannot prosper as the White Jews of the United States have prospered because they know who they are. God spoke to me and let me know that we were Jews. He let me know this very early when I got saved/born again, but I did not understand, as I mentioned earlier. God showed me in a dream, everywhere I looked, signs with the name Zephaniah on it. They were everywhere I looked. I thought that God wanted me to read what the Prophet of Holy Scriptures/Bible had said about the end times. At that time, God was showing me many things about the end times. So, I read the Book of Zephaniah to see what it was saying about the end times. I had read that Book before and when I read it again it yielded no additional revelation to me. I now know after many years what God wanted me to see. The reason I did not see it is because of the brain washing, the mind control witchcraft, of Black People in the United States.

Black People, including me, have been brained washed, to only think that the Jews in the United States are only White. God spoke to Prophetess Sylvia Franklin, my wife, and said, that there were no white people saved during Biblical times. The reason that there are now White Jews, is because when God scattered his people among the nations, some of them went into Europe and mixed with and married the Europeans.

Deuteronomy Ch. 28, V. 64
"And the LORD shall scatter thee among all people, from the one and of earth even unto the other . . ."

The Jews, who were scattered into Europe, entangled themselves with Europeans in sex and marriage. Over the years these Jews began to look white. They even changed their names so no one would be able to associate them with the Jews. They even took on their culture. This is why you find so many sodomites/homosexuals among these White Jews.

Let us get back to why God wanted me to read the Book of Zephaniah. The reason God wanted me to read the Book of Zephaniah is in Chapter 1, Verse 1.

Zephaniah Ch. 1, V. 1
"The word of the LORD which came unto Zephaniah the son of Cushi, the son of Geddliah, the son of Amariah, the son of Hizkiah, in the days of Josiah the son of Amon, king of Judiah."

There it is right there! You don't see it. Zephaniah was the son of Cushi. Cushi was an Ethiopian. Zephaniah was a Black man. Zephaniah a Prophet of the Holy Bible was a Black man. Part of the Holy Scriptures was written by a Black man.

Black People who have been brained washed to think that we had no important heritage, actually had heritage as being God's Holy People! Black People were important enough to be part of God's word for mankind. How in the world after all of these years with all of this preaching, including by Black Preachers, of the Holy Bible/Scriptures, that this has not been "revealed". This "revelation" has been hidden because of the mind control witchcraft that has been established across the earth on Black People. Satan, himself, has established it through the vessels of the White Slave owners & Ku Klux Klan. The (KKK) Ku Klux Klan is a coward terrorist organization that was established after the Civil War. It is a United States' home grown terrorist organization. The largest and one of the first terrorist groups in the world. It was established by those White folks who were sympathetic to having slaves in the United States. Their main goal was to intimidate Black People, ex-Slaves, Black Jews, to take back what they had loss in the Civil War. The makeup of their intimidation was to steal, kill and destroy. Of course, they would use the same tactics of their father the Devil/Satan. Part of the KKK's strategy was to do things under cover. They would cowardly hide their faces with a hood. A group of them hiding their faces with guns would team up against a single armless Black man. Another part of their strategy was to use the same mind control witchcraft/wizardry that they had used as slave owners.

After God opened up my eyes to this hidden "revelation" of Black People being in the Scriptures, God showed me other instances of the Scriptures where Black People were prominent among his people and the Scriptures. God directed me to the scriptures that showed that Black People were even associated with the Tribe of Judah. Jesus the Christ, the Messiah, was of the Tribe of Judah.

<u>Zachariah Ch. 6, Vs. 10,11 & 14</u>
"Take of them of the captivity even of Heldai, of Tobijah, and Jedaoah, which are come from Babylon, and come thou the same day, and go into the house of Josiah the son of Zephaniah; Then take silver and gold, and make crowns, and set them upon the head of Joshua the son of Josedeck, the high priest; And the crowns shall be to Helem, and to Tobijah, and to Jedaiah, and to Hen the son of Zephaniah, for a memorial in the temple of the Lord."

Here are a few of the prominent names in the Holy Scriptures/Bible of Black Men & Black Women:

1. Zephaniah
2. Josiah
3. Jedihu
4. Nethaniah
5. Shelemiah/Meshelemiah
6. Cush
7. Cushi

8. Amariah
9. Gedaliah
10. Hizkiah/Hezikiah
11. Jeduthun
12. Pashur
13. Ahikam
14. Zechariah
15. Ebedmelech
16. Midian
17. Jucal
18. Kenaz
19. Othniel
20. Caleb
21. Jephunneh
22. Jethro
23. Sheba
24. Dedan
25. Jokshan
26. Medan
27. Zimran
28. Ashurim
29. Letushin
30. Luummin
31. Ephah
32. Epher
33. Hanoch
34. Abidah
35. Eldaah
36. Keturah

37. Neariah
38. Candace
39. Zipporah
40. Others

These are just some of the Black People of the Holy Scriptures/Bible and most of them were of the covenant with God. The covenant with Abraham, Isaac and Jacob. Below are some of the scriptures that prove the assertion of the Black People mentioned above found in the Holy Scriptures/Bible.

Zephaniah Ch. 1, V. 1
"The word of the Lord which came unto Zephaniah the son of Cushi, the son of Gedaliah, the son of Amariah, the son of Hizkiah, in the days of Josiah the son of Amon, king of Judah."

Zechariah Ch. 6, Vs. 10,11 & 14
"Take of them of the captivity, even Heldai, of Tobijah, and Jedaiah, which are come from Babylon, and come thou the same day, and go into the house of Josiah the son of Zephaniah; Then take silver and gold, and make crowns, and set them upon the head of Joshua the son of Josedech, the high priest; And the crowns shall be to Helem, and to Tobijah, and to Jedaiah, and to Hen the son of Zephaniah, for a memorial in the temple of the Lord."

II Kings Ch. 22, V. 1

"JOSIAH was eight years old when he began to reign, and he reigned thirty and one years in Jerusalem. And his mother's name was Jedidah, the daughter of Adaiah of Boscath."

Numbers Ch. 12, V. 1

"AND Miriam and Aaron spake against Moses because of the Ethiopian woman whom he had married: for he had married an Ethiopian woman."

Exodus Ch. 3, V. 1 & Ch. 2, V. 1

"Now Moses kept the flock of Jethro his father in law, the priest of Midian . . . And Moses was content to dwell with the man: and he gave Moses Zipporah his daughter."

Jeremiah Ch. 36, Vs. 1,14 & 21

"AND it came to pass in the fourth year of Jehoikim the son of Josiah king of Judah, that this word came unto Jeremiah, saying, Take thee a roll and write therein all the words that I have spoken unto thee . . . Therefore all the princes sent Jehudi, the son of Nethaniah, the son of Shelemiah, the son of Cushi, unto Baruch, saying, Take in thine hand the roll of wherein thou hast read . . . So the king sent Jehudi to fetch the roll; and he took it out of Elishama the scribe's chamber. And Jehudi read it in ears of the king, and in the ears of the princes which stood beside the king."

Jehudi was an Ethiopian officer. Nethaniah was a Levite teacher.

II Chronicles Ch.17, Vs.3 & 8

"And the LORD was with Jehoshaphat, . . . he sent Levites, even Shemaiah, and Nethaniah, and Zebadiah, and Asahel, and Shemiramoth, and Abonijah, and Tobijah, and Tobadoni, Levites; and with them Elishima and Jehoram, priests."

I Chronicles Ch. 25, Vs. 1,2 & 3

"Moreover David and the captains of the host separated to the service of the sons of Asaph, and of Heman, and Jeduthun, who should prophesy with harps, with psalteries, and with cymbals: and the number of the workmen according to their service was: of the sons of Asaph: Zaccur, and Joseph, and Nethaniah, and Aserlah, the sons of Asaph under the hands of Asaph, which prophesied according to the order of the king. Of Jeduthun: the sons of Jeduthun; Hedaliah, and Zeri, and Jeshaiah, Hashabiah, and Mattithiah, six, under the hands of their father Jeduthun, who prophesied with a harp, to give thanks and to praise the LORD."

I Chronicles Ch. 23, Vs. 6,12,13 & 19

"And David divided them into courses among the sons of Levi, namely, Gershon, Kohath, and Marari. The sons of Kohath; Amram, Izhar, Hebron, and Uzziel, four. The sons of Amram; Aaron and Moses . . . Of the sons of Hebron; Jeriah the first, <u>Amariah the second,</u> Jahaziel the third, and Jekameam the fourth."

This indicates that Moses could have been Black.

<u>I Chronicles Ch. 25, Vs. 6-31</u>
"All these were under the hands of their father for song in the house of the LORD, according to the kings order to Asaph, Jeduthun, and Heman. So the number of them, with their brethren that were instructed in the songs of the LORD, even all that were cunning, was two hundred fourscore and eight. And they cast lots, ward against ward, as well the small and the great, the teachers as the scholar. Now the first lot came forth for Asaph to Joseph: the second to Gedaliah, who with his brethren and sons were twelve . . ."

<u>I Chronicles Ch. 2, Vs. 1 & 2</u>
"Concerning the divisions of the porters: Of the Korhites was Meshelemiah the son of Kore, of the sons of Asaph. And the sons of Meshelemiah were Zechariah the first born . . ."

Meshelemiah is the same as Shelemiah.

<u>I Chronicles Ch. 26, Vs. 14</u>
"And the lot eastward fell to Shelemiah. Then Zechariah his son, a wise counselor . . ."

Jeremiah Ch. 38, Vs. 1,5,7 & 13

"THEN Shephatiah the son of Mattan, and Gedaliah the son of Pashur, and Jucal the son of Shelemiah and Pashur the son of Malchiah, heard the words that Jeremiah had spoken . . . Then Zedekiah the king said, Behold he is in your hand . . . Now when Ebedmelech the Ethiopian, one of the eunuchs which was in the king's house . . . drew up Jeremiah with cards, and took him up out of the dungeon . . ."

Numbers Ch. 31, Vs. 1,18 & 35

"AND the LORD spake unto Moses, saying, Avenge the children of Israel of the Midianites . . . But all the women children that have not known a man by lying with, keep alive for yourself. And thirty and two thousand persons in all, of women . . ."

Here we see that 32,000 Black women were joined to the Jews.

Judges Ch. 1, V. 16

"And the children of the Kenite, Moses' father in law, went up out of the city of palm trees with the children of Judah into the wilderness of Judah, which lieth south of Arad; and they went and dwelt among the people."

Here we see Black People being joined with the Tribe of Judah.

Numbers Ch. 32, Vs. 10,11 & 12
"And the LORD's anger was kindled . . . saying, Surely none of the men that came up out of Egypt, from twenty years old and upward, shall see the land which I sware unto Abraham, unto Isaac, and unto Jacob; because they have not wholly followed me; Save Caleb the son of Jephunneh the Kenezite, and Joshua the son of Nun."

The Kenites were the same as the Kenezites, which were Black.

Numbers Ch. 13, Vs. 1,2,3 & 6
"AND the LORD spake unto Moses, saying, Send thou men, that they may search the land of Cannan, which I give unto the children of Israel: of every tribe of their fathers shall ye send a man, everyone a ruler among them. And Moses by the commandment of the LORD sent them from the wilderness of Paran: all those men were heads of the children of Israel. Of the tribe of Judah, Caleb the son of Jephunneh."

Here we see Caleb, a Black Man, was the head of the Tribe of Judah.

Joshua Ch. 15, Vs. 13 & 17
"And unto Caleb the son of Jephunneh . . . And Othniel the son of Kenaz, the brother of Caleb . . ."

Othniel was the first Judge of Israel.

Judges Ch. 3, Vs. 9-11

"And the children of Israel cried unto the LORD, the LORD raised up a deliverer to the children of Israel, who delivered them, even Othniel the son of Kenaz, Caleb's younger brother. And the Spirit of the LORD came upon him, and he judged Israel, and went out to war . . . and his hand prevailed . . . And the land had rest forty years. And Othniel the son of Kenaz died."

Judges Ch. 3, V. 20

"And they gave Hebron unto Caleb, as Moses said . . ."

This shows that Caleb is the same Caleb that was with Moses and is the son of Jephunneh.

Genesis Ch. 25, Vs. 1-4

"THEN Abraham took a wife, and her name was Keturah. And she bare him Zimram, and Jokshan, and Medan, and Midian, and Ishbak, and Shuah. And Jokshan begat Sheba, and Dedan. And the sons of Dedan were Asshurim, and Letushim, and Leummin. And the sons of Midian: Ephah, and Epher, and Hanoch, and Abidah, and Eldaah. All these were children of Keturah."

Keturah, Abraham's wife after Sarah died, his second wife, was Black.

Joshua Ch. 14, Vs. 6,9,13 & 14

". . . Caleb the son of Jephunneh the Kenezite . . . And Moses sware . . . saying, surely the land . . . shall be thy inheritance . . . And Joshua blessed him, and unto Caleb the son of Jephunneh, Hebron for an inheritance. Hebron therefore became the inheritance of Caleb the son of Jephunneh the Kenezite . . ."

Kenite is the same as Kenezite.

Judges Ch. 1, Vs.16

"And the children of the Kenite, Moses' father in law . . ."

Acts Ch. 8, Vs. 26 & 27

"And the angel of the Lord spake until Philip, saying, Arise, and go toward the south unto the way that goeth down from Jerusalem unto Gaza which is desert. And he rose and went; and, behold, a man under Candace queen of the Ethiopians who had the charge of all her treasure, and had come down to Jerusalem for to worship."

Queen Candace of Ethiopia, a Black Woman & her treasurer, were worshipping during the feast associated with the Passover in Jerusalem. They were not the only Black people worshipping during that time.

Some years went by after God showed me the signs saying Zephaniah; God then told me that Black People in the United States, Offspring of the Slaves in the United States, were Jews. God even told us some astonishing things that we would not have even thought that God would say. These things we will not reveal at this time. Recently, beginning in the summer of the Year 2011, as we call it, God spoke to a young prophet, Darien Foster, under my Apostleship, and said that every Black Person in the United States is a Jew. This was a confirmation of what God had earlier told me that I mentioned.

The Scriptures again, give validity to God's and my assertion that Black People, the Offspring of Slaves, in the United States are Jews. The Holy Scriptures in the Book of Revelation refer to the United States as Babylon the Great. God, also, has appeared unto me to tell me this is so. God appeared unto me in a dream. We were up high looking down on the earth. God was on my left side. All of a sudden God showed me a very large and thick book. God let me know that this book contained every event of the history of mankind, from the Book of Genesis through the Book of Revelation. God then opened up the very large and thick book. He opened up the book to the back part of the back half of the book. He began to turn the pages of the book. As he turned the page, there appeared, us looking downward, a vision. The vision was what was written on the printed pages of the book. As God turned the page, another vision appeared before us as we looked down toward it. This vision also was what was on the printed page. These printed words on the pages and the associated visions were things of the future. God again turned the page going toward the end of the book. Just as before, there was another vision of the future. He turned to the next page and there was another vision of the future. On and on, God did this and a vision would appear. I will not tell at this time all of what God showed me of the future. I will, however, say this. As God turned the printed page, I saw a vision, as was on the printed page, missiles flying through the sky. They were arrayed in pattern. They looked similar in pattern to winter migration of birds/fowls. There were many of the missiles. One pattern after another flying in the sky headed somewhere. There were nuclear and poison gas missiles. God then turned the page. Again there was a vision. This time there appeared fire and explosions happening somewhere on earth. Great fires and great explosions were happening. God again turned the page. There, again, what was on the printed page, a vision appeared. This time in the vision, as was on the printed page, were large fowls. Several to many of them. They looked very bad. They were filthy looking. They were vomiting. They looked retarded. God showed me where what I had seen was located in the Holy Scriptures/ Bible. He took me to Revelation Chapter 18, Verses 1 and 2.

<u>Revelation Ch. 8, Vs. 1 & 2</u>

"And after these things I saw another angel come down from heaven, having great power; and the earth was lightened with his glory. And he cried mightily with a strong voice, saying, Babylon the great is fallen, is fallen, and is become the habitation of devils, and the hold of every foul spirit, and a cage of every unclean and hateful bird."

After God had me to read these scriptures, He said that the filthy, vomiting and retarded looking fowls that I saw in the vision are these unclean and hateful birds that are in these scriptures. Then God said that the birds are called unclean and hateful because of the nuclear contamination and poison gas release associated with the missiles and explosions and fires that I saw in the visions. God then said that Babylon the Great is the United States. The explosions and fires were happening to the United States in the vision that I saw. This is the Destruction of the United States that will be carried out by Pope John Paul II and Former President Bill Clinton. This will be done to silence the saints of God in the United States. This will happen immediately after the Great Tribulation. The First Resurrection, the so-called Rapture, will take place in moments before the missile attacks occur. Refer to our Books:

1.   "Judgment Of The United States"
2.   "United States In The Bible"

3.   "Words From God, By God Appearing To Us
      Or Just Talking To Us, For The End Times"

As a side issue, let me mention this. I said that the
United States will be destroyed by Former President
Bill Clinton & Pope John Paul II. Pope John Paul II is
not dead. That was a fake death and funeral that they
had for him over in the Vatican, in Rome, Italy. He is the
so-called anti-Christ, Beast. The one who will require
all those on the earth to take his 666 mark and worship
him. The Pope's name, Pope John Paul II, is Carol Josef
Wojtyla. His name is equal to 666. Former President
Bill Clinton is the other beast of Revelation Chapter 13.
He is also called the False Prophet. He is the one that
is going to administer the deceptive will of Pope John
Paul II. God has told me over (30) thirty times that that
Pope is the Beast, the so-called anti-Christ. Refer to
our Books:

1.   "The Name Of The (Anti-Christ) Beast And
      666 Identification"
2.   "Who Is The (False Prophet) Second Beast"
3.   "Words From God, By God Appearing To Us
      Or Just Talking To Us, For The End Times"

Now let me show you the significance of the United
States being Babylon the Great and how it is connected
with Black People of United States being Jews. Babylon
the Great is also called the Whore, Harlot or Woman.

Revelation Ch. 17, Vs. 15 & 16

"And he said unto me, The waters which thou sawest, where the whore sitteth, are peoples, and multitudes, and nations and tongues. And the ten horns which thou sawest upon the beast, these shall hate the whore, and shall make her desolate and naked, and shall eat her flesh, and burn her with fire."

Revelation Ch. 17, Vs. 5 & 6

"And upon her forehead was a name written, MYSTERY, BABYLON THE GREAT, THE MOTHER OF HARLOTS AND ABOMINATIONS OF THE EARTH. And I saw the woman, drunken with blood of saints, and with the blood of the martyrs of Jesus . . ."

The United States, Babylon The Great, is also known as that "Great City" in the Book of Revelation of the Holy Scriptures/Bible.

Revelation Ch. 17, V. 18

"And the woman which thou sawest is that great city, which reigneth over the kings of the earth."

Revelation Ch. 18, Vs. 9 & 10

"And the kings of the earth, who have committed fornication and lived deliciously with her, shall bewail her, and lament for her, when they shall see the smoke of her burning. Standing afar off for the fear of her torment, saying, Alas, alas, that <u>great city</u> Babylon, that mighty city! For in one hour is thy judgment come."

Revelation Ch. 18, Vs. 20 & 24
"Rejoice over her, thou heaven and ye holy apostles and prophets; for God hath avenged you on her. And in her was found the blood of prophets, and saints, and all that were slain upon the earth."

Revelation Ch. 18, Vs. 16-19
". . . that <u>great city</u>, that was clothed in fine linen, and purple, and scarlet, and decked with gold, and precious stones, and pearls: For in one hour so great riches is come to nought. And every shipmaster, and all the company in ships, and sailers, and as many trade by sea, stood afar off. And cried when they saw the smoke of her burning, saying, What city is like unto this <u>great city</u>, wherein were made rich all that had ships in the sea . . ."

You might say, but I still don't see the connection with Black People of the United States being Jews. Look at Revelation Chapter 11. There it says that the United Sates, Babylon The Great, that <u>Great City</u>, is also referred to as the modern day Egypt of the Egypt of old.

Revelation Ch. 11, Vs. 3,7 & 8
"And I will give power unto my two witnesses . . . And when they shall have finished their testimony, the beast

that ascendeth out of the bottomless pit shall make war against them, and shall overcome them, and kill them. And their dead bodies shall lie in the street of the <u>great city</u>, which spiritually is called Sodom and Egypt, where also our Lord was crucified."

You might say, the <u>great city</u> is talking about Jerusalem because that is where Jesus was crucified. No. No. The point is that Jesus was crucified in the street. The Street is the key, not Jerusalem. The Lord was crucified in the street. The "Great City" here in Chapter 11 is also the "Great City" of Chapter 17 and Chapter 18, written by the same author, Apostle John. Jerusalem is <u>not</u> referred to as the <u>Great City</u> anywhere in the Holy Scriptures/ Bible. Jerusalem is referred to as the "Holy City", "City of God" or "City of David". Even in the Book of Revelation.

<u>Revelation Ch. 21, V. 2</u>
"And I John saw the <u>holy city</u>, new Jerusalem, coming down from God out of heaven, prepared as a bride adorned for her husband."

<u>Psalm 46, V. 4</u>
"There is a river, the streams whereof shall make glad the city of God, the holy place of the tabernacles of the most High."

<u>Nehemiah Ch. 11, V. 1</u>
". . . dwell in Jerusalem the holy city . . ."

<u>Psalm 87, Vs. 2 & 3</u>
"The LORD loveth the gates of Zion more than all the dwellings of Jacob. Glorious things are spoken of thee, O city of God."

<u>I Kings Ch. 2, V. 10</u>
"So David slept with his fathers, and was buried in the city of David."

You might say, ok, but how is the United States a city. First of all God said it was that <u>great city</u>. I give clear and detail explanation of this in our Books:

1. "United States In The Bible"
2. "Judgment Of The United States"

I will, however, say these few words regarding the United States being a city. The United States will lose its sovereignty as a country. Refer to our Book "New York City Becomes The Capitol Of The New World Order". It, as I have said in another of our books, will be placed under the United Nations, with Former President Bill Clinton being its President along with the other countries of the world. Another thing that points to the United States losing its sovereignty, is that right now, as

I write this book, parts of the United States are owned by other countries in business ventures and otherwise.

Well, you might say, I yet do not see how Black People in the United States are Jews. Well, God said concerning his People, the Jews, being scattered, that they would be taken captive by Egypt. He, further, said as he prophesied, that the Jews being taken captive into Egypt will go there by ships. God's people of old did not go into Egypt by ships. The only people who were taken captive into the modern day Egypt, the United States, by ship were the Black Slaves from Africa.

<u>Deuteronomy Ch. 28, V. 68</u>
"And the LORD shall bring thee into Egypt again with ships, by the way whereof I spake and there ye shall be sold unto your enemies for bondmen and bondwomen, and no man shall buy you."

"No man shall buy you" means that no one will buy you out of slavery.

The Black People brought on ships from Africa were Jews, God's People. The Offspring of The Black People from Africa brought into the United States as Slaves were and are Jews, God's people.

Let me say this. What is in the Holy Scriptures/Bible of the Old Testament has a spiritual counterpart in the

New Testament. For instance, the Lamb that was slain in the Old Testament, was Jesus Christ of the New Testament; Moses the Deliver, was Jesus the Savior; the children of Israel, the New Testament Church; Egypt the super power of that time, holding bondage the Jews, was the United States, the super power of this time, holding bondage the Jews.

<u>Note this</u>. The Jews in Egypt of old, were captive for (400) four hundred years, they were delivered out of captivity without them having to fight any battle. The Black Slaves taken captive in the United States were not required to fight any battle for their freedom. God did it. As God did it in Egypt of old. God controls everything. God caused his people's enemies to fight among themselves, North against South.

<u>Isaiah Ch. 19, Vs. 2 & 3</u>
"And I will set the Egyptians against the Egyptians: and they shall fight every one against his neighbour; city against city, and kingdom against kingdom. And the spirit of Egypt shall fail in the midst thereof; and I will destroy the counsel thereof: and they shall seek to the idols, and to the charmers, and to them that have familiar spirits, and to the wizards."

These above prophecies in Isaiah and Deuteronomy are far after Moses' day. There was no captivity of the children of Israel by the Egyptians in Biblical days other than the time of Moses. These are prophecies concerning the United States. In the captivity of Egypt of old, the Egyptians did not fight against each other.

It is time for truth to be revealed. This what we are about to say is shameful, but in keeping with truth it must be said. Another probable similarity of the Slaves and their Offspring of the United States to the Slaves of Egypt of Old, is what I call the Dathan spirit. In the time of slavery of God's People in Egypt of Old, there was one called Dathan. Even though it is not in the Scriptures, "The Ten Commandments" Movie showed Dathan as one who conspired with Egypt against his own People. The movie indicated that Dathan enhanced the ability of Egypt to keep his People under slavery to get a token of reward and affection from Egypt. To get "a pat on the back". Even though it is not in the Scriptures, it is very likely that such was the case. The Dathan spirit of this time has been coined as the "Uncle Tom". It started during slavery when the slave would spy on his fellow slaves for the slave master/owner. Sometimes the spy was promoted by letting him/her work in the house. In the case of the women, sometimes the slave master/ owner would have sex with her. Sometimes it was rape, but sometimes it was not. Sometimes the woman would get pregnant and have the slave master's/owner's child. This is one of the reasons you find so many that are of light complexion among us. After slavery there was an effort doing the latter 1800's through the first half of the 1900's, to eradicate the dark skin from the Black People through Natural Selection. This was a self-imposed effort due to the mind control witchcraft. If you could get your subjects to want to be like you, then the subjects are less likely to rise up against you. All the subjects will want to do is to imitate you. It is mind control witchcraft. A like effort had been carried out in Mexico, Cuba, Brazil and the other areas in the Americas where slaves had been brought from Africa. You might say that this sounds kind of far fetching. Well, the Scriptures back us up. In the spiritual Egypt, the United States, the Great City, you see the influence of witchcraft.

Isaiah Ch. 19, Vs. 2 & 3

"And I will set the Egyptians against the Egyptians, and they shall fight every one against his brother . . . and they shall seek to the idols, and to the chambers, and to them that have familiar spirits, and to the wizards."

Revelation Ch. 18, V. 23

". . . for by thy sorceries were all nations deceived."

Matthew Ch. 10, V.26

". . . for there is nothing covered, that shall not be revealed; and hid, that shall not be known."

<u>John Ch. 8, V. 32</u>

"And ye shall know the truth and the truth shall make you free."

You might ask, are all Black People across the earth Jews? No. No. No. In order for the Black People in Africa to be sold into slavery, there had to be other Black Africans who sold them to the White slave owners. The Black People in Africa who were not Jews, resented the Black People who were Jews. They, the non-Jews, of course were Satan's children and therefore hated God's people even as the Slave owners, who were Satan's children, hated the Black Jews. The Black People who were not Jews, the heathens, conquered the Tribes of the Black People who were Jews and sold them into slavery. Satan, of course, was behind it all, but God allowed it to happen because of His people disobedience to Him. The analogous attitude and effort of the Black People, Satan's children, who sold the Black Jews into slavery, are the present Muslim groups in Africa who are against the Christian and so-called Christian Africans. If the Muslims could sale the Christians or the so-called Christians into slavery, they would be sold.

We believe that this book will bring to pass a prophesy that God gave to my wife, Prophetess Sylvia Franklin. God prophesied through her several years ago and said that there will be Black Muslims in the United States who will get saved. God showed that these ex-Muslims would be praising Jesus. Among these ex-Muslims was Louis Farrakhan.

We believe that through this book, that many Black People outside the United States will get saved/born again. This includes the Offspring of those Black People who jumped ship when the Slaves were being brought to the United States. Those that are in Haiti, Cuba, Virgin Island, Bahamas, Dominican Republic and others.

Not all of the Black Jews that were in Africa were capture and sold into slavery. We believe that this book will also get many in Africa saved/born again.

Through this book the White Slave owners' mind control witchcraft will be broken off the Black People of the United States. This book sets us free. This book will allow certain Black People in the United States to be saved. Also, non-Blacks, even some Whites, will get saved due to this book.

There are many Black People in the United States. God has, however, said that only (148,000) one hundred forty eight thousand souls will be saved in the United States in these last days. Remember the dream that I told you about where I saw the visions with God being on my left side? Well, one of the things that God showed me in the visions, was the number that would be saved in the United States. How many would be in the First

Resurrection, the so-called Rapture. That number would be (148,000) one hundred forty eight thousand. We suggest that everyone who can, figure out a way to leave the United States. This will enhance your chance to be saved. To be in the First Resurrection, the so-called Rapture. It also enhances the chances of those who cannot leave to be saved. We know that all saints will not leave the United States because there will be saints killed here.

Revelation Ch. 18, V. 24

"And in her was found the blood of prophets, and of saints, and of all that were slain upon the earth."

This exit strategy that I mentioned is in line with God's written word. In the Bible/Scriptures, God told his people to leave when pending destruction was going to come to the place where his were located. It was true for Lot and his household in Sodom.

Genesis Ch. 19, Vs. 1,12 & 13

"And there came two angels to Sodom at even; and Lot sat in the gate of Sodom: and Lot seeing them rose up to meet them; and he bowed himself with his face to the ground; And the men said unto Lot, Hast thou here any besides? son in law, and thy sons, and thy daughters, and whatsoever thou hast in the city, bring them out of this place: For we will destroy this place . . . the LORD has sent us to destroy it."

Also, even in the Book of Revelation, even God talking concerning Babylon the Great, the United States, God says to his people, come out before destruction. This is also talking about exit due to the First Resurrection, the so-called Rapture. Nevertheless, God gets his people out of a destructive situation.

Revelation Ch. 18, Vs. 4 & 5
"And I heard another voice from heaven, saying, Come out of her, my people, that ye be not partakers of her sins, and that ye receive not of her plagues. Therefore shall her plagues come in one day, death, and mourning, and famine; and she shall be utterly burnt with fire: for strong is the Lord God who judgeth her."

Let us get back to the main subject, Black People in the United States are Jews. God has given his people special wisdom and ability. That is why the White Jews have accomplished so much in this country in every facet of the society. Among these Jews are:

1. Albert Einstein
2. Frank Oppenheimer
3. Carl Sagan
4. Judith Resnik
5. David Wolf
6. Louis Bradeis
7. Ruth Bader Ginsburg
8. Shephen Breyer

9. Elena Kagan
10. Aaron Brown
11. Bernard Goldberg
12. Mike Wallace
13. Barbara Walters
14. Frank Rich
15. Louis Boudreau
16. Hank Greenburg
17. Sandy Koufax
18. Rachel Maddow
19. Ezra Klein
20. (many others)

The Black Jews of the United States have excelled in every area of the society that we were allowed to participate in. After slavery, Black People were even yet greatly discriminated against. However, in those areas of the society that we were allowed to participate in, Black People excelled. God has blessed Black People with strong bodies of good health and brilliant minds. God blessed us especially so because of all of the discrimination that we had to endure. The only things that Black People were allowed to do with the possibility of gaining riches were in music and sports. Well, Black People were/are the best. As time passed, other areas of the society were penetrated by the Black Jews. Like as with the sports and music, the Black Jews excelled. They excelled as engineers, doctors, scientists, lawyers, teachers, politicians, etc. Up until about the

1970's, Black Jews philosophy of life was to be at least twice as good as the best White person in a particular job or profession. This way if you were at least twice as good, then you could get a job competing with the lowest of White People.

You might say, if God allowed the children of Israel, the Jews, to be taken into slavery, then that means God had forsaken them. God, you might say, then would not bless them with any kind of special qualities. No, no, that is not true.

<u>Ezekiel Ch. 11, V. 16</u>
". . . and although I have scattered them among the countries, yet will I be to them as a little sanctuary in the countries where they shall come."

After the civil war in the United States, there was great institutionalize discrimination against the ex-Slaves, Black Jews, like the world had never seen. A lot of this discrimination exists to this very day. The discrimination was based totally on the fact that we were and are Black. It was and is Racism. Over the years there were and are some descent White folks who were and are against this evil of Racism. So these descent White folks combined forces with the Black People to try to eradicate the United States of this evil. They along with other efforts accomplish some things toward this end, even resulting in a Black man getting elected as President, President Barack Obama. However, the root and seed of Racism yet exist. The reason this evil yet exist is because of something you might not have ever considered. It yet exist because the descent White folks and the Black People will not tell the truth about what Racism is. They the descent White folks and Black People have been unintentional co-conspirators with this evil of Racism. They, the descent White folks and Black People, because of their timid definition of Racism has allowed it to continue. If the true definition of Racism had been espoused, the manifestation of Racism would have disappeared in a flash. It might not have left out of the hearts of people, but the outward manifestation of it would have disappeared. Once this definition of Racism had been established it would have vanished.

The descent White folks would not define Racism as what it is for embarrassing reasons. The Black People would not define Racism as what it is because they were afraid of embarrassing and losing the support of the descent White folks. So, the conspiracy continues.

Racism is nothing more or less than sin. Racism is jealousy and envy! God spoke to me and said this is what it is. Racism is, therefore, White People being jealous and envious of Black People. If the truth had been told about Racism, it would have been eradicated, at least in outward manifestation. If Racism was yet in the heart of White People, they surely would not have it to be known that they were jealous and envious of the Black Person or People.

Listed below are some triumphant Black People in the United States, in spite of the Racism. Some of them listed you probably never have heard of. Many to most of the times, the accomplishments of the Black Jews were stolen by the White People. Before we go any further, let us say this. We are about to provide a list of Black People, Black Jews, who have been triumphant in the United States, in spite of the systematic discrimination. We know that there are many hundreds of names that are not on our list who should be. In fact, you might be more worthy to be on the list than some who are on it. We apologize beforehand for our omission. A few of the triumphant Black Jews of the United States:

1. Barack Hussein Obama, President
2. Michelle Obama, 1st Black First Lady
3. Eric Holder, 1st Black Attorney General
4. Colon Power, 1st Black Secretary Of Defense, [1st Secretary Of State]
5. Henry Neal Tolbert, Real Estate Tycoon
6. Selena Tolbert, Mother & Community Servant
7. Hank Aaron, Baseball Home Run King
8. Jackie Robinson, 1st Black Baseball Player
9. Muhammad Ali, Boxing Champion
10. Count Basie, Music Composer

11. Martin Luther King Jr., Only Black With A Holiday
12. Edna Abrams, Single Parent & Community Leader
13. Rufus Tolbert, Genius Carpenter (at 14 built a house), Electrician, Plumber, Mechanic & Farmer
14. LeGrant Wright, Ph D Educator
15. Fred Jones, Colonel In U. S. [Marines]
16. Shirley Jones, Educator, Int. Trav. & Entrepreneur
17. Joe Neal Tolbert, Educator, Historian & Artist
18. Adam Clayton Powell Jr., Congressman
19. Shirley Chilsom, Congresswoman
20. Booker T. Washington, Tuskegee Inst. Uni. Founder
21. George Washington Carver, Scientist
22. Sam Jones, 1st Black Major Of Mobile
23. Malcolm X, Black Liberation Leader
24. Andrew Young, 1st Black Ambassador
25. Harriet Tubman, Abolitionist
26. Willie Mays, Hall Of Fame Baseball Player
27. Gary Cooper, Mayor Of Atlanta
28. Sidney Poitier, Actor
29. Harry Belefonte, Singer & Actor
30. Bill Cosby, 1st Black To Star On TV Show
31. Satchel Paige, Baseball Player
32. Julian Bond, Congressman
33. Quincy Jones, Music Composer

34. Frederick E. Douglas, Abolitionist &1st B. Politician
35. Mahalia Jackson, Gospel Singer
36. Maya Angelou, Poet
37. Thurgood Marshall, 1st Black Supreme Ct. Justice
38. Joe Brown, TV Show Judge
39. Alex Haley, Author
40. Rosa Park, Leader Of 1st Bus Boycot
41. Rap Brown, Leader Of Black Liberation ·
42. Jessie Owens, 1st Track Champion
43. Doug Williams, 1st Black QB To Win Super Bowl
44. Bill Russell, Champion Basketball Player
45. Jessie Jackson, Leader Of Black Equality
46. Al Sharpton, TV Political Anchor & BE Activist
47. Annie Mae Flowers, Single Parent
48. Spike Lee, Movie Maker
49. Tyler Perry, Movie Maker
50. Cicely Tyson, Actress
51. Maxine Walters, Congresswoman
52. Angela Davis, Leader Of Black Liberation
53. William A. Tumlin, Apostle/Bishop
54. William J. Seymour, Started Pentecostal Revival
55. Willie McCovery, Hall Of Fame Baseball Player
56. Tavis Smiley, TV Talk Show Host

57. Denzel Washington, Actor
58. Dick Gregory, Political Activist For B. Equality
59. Ozzie Davis Jr., Actor
60. Della Reese, Actress
61. Rudy Dee Davis, Actress
62. James Earl Jones, Actor
63. Ella Fitzgerald, Singer
64. Joe Louis, Boxing Champion
65. Marian Anderson, Opera Singer
66. Dred Scot, Famous Slave
67. Gwen Iffer, TV News Anchor
68. William E. B. Du Bois, Founder Of NAACP
69. Oprah Winfrey, TV Media Host & Founder
70. John Johnson, Founder Of Jet & Ebony Magazines
71. Barbara Jordon, Congresswoman
72. Bernard Shaw, TV News Anchor
73. Morgan Freeman, Actor
74. Kenneth Rocker, Executive Electrical Engineer
75. Samuel Cahoon, Executive Electrical Engineer
76. William Foy Robinson, Executive Elec. Engineer
77. Lucius Monroe, Executive Electrical Engineer
78. Willie Wortham, Colonel In U. S. Navy
79. Samuel White, Ph D Professor (Elec. Engineering)
80. Lawrence Slatter, Computer Engineering Expert
81. Leroy Rhodes, Executive Electrical Engineer

82. Fred Stone, Computer Engineering Expert
83. Benny James, Executive Electrical Engineer
84. Ronald Boyd, Executive Electrical Engineer
85. Eutice Blakely, Executive Electrical Engineer
86. Robert Smith, Executive Electrical Engineer
87. Elmer C. Stovall, Executive Mechanical Engineer
88. William Still, Abolitionist
89. Wilma Rudolph, Track Champion
90. Eddie Robinson, Most Wins Football Coach
91. Joseph Levert, Nuclear & Mechani. Eng. Professor
92. Ernest Grant, Electrical Engineering Professor
93. Warren Clayton, Ph D Elec. Engineering Professor
94. Henry Louis Gates Jr., Profes., Hist. & Docu. Host
95. Tom Joyner, Radio Broadcaster
96. John Louis, Congressman
97. James E. Clyburn, Congressman
98. Duke Ellington, Music Composer
99. Willie Brown, Jr., Mayor Of Los Angeles
100. Ben Carson, Brain Surgeon
101. Robert Henry Lawrence, Jr., 1st Black Astronaut
102. Regina M. Benjamin, 1st Black Surgeon General
103. Lester Holt, News Anchor
104. Benjamin Hooks, Head Of The FCC
105. Vernon Jordon, Entrepreneur

106. Nat Turner, Slave Freedom Fighter
107. Ervin Tolbert, World War II Vet & House Builder
108. Curtis Tolbert, World War II Vet & Farmer
109. Freda Borden, Mother & Pioneer In NT Job Market
110. Verna Cephas, Mother & Community Servant
111. Joyce Voncile Tolbert, Educator & Com. Servant
112. Erma Jean Tolbert, Educator & Com. Organizer
113. Nadene Showers, Educator & Mathematician
114. Robin Roberts, TV News Anchor
115. Judge Greg Mathis, TV Show Judge

It is absolutely amazing that such as the above list could be possible in a situation where the people had been stripped of language, family, identity and heritage. It had to be God with such a people! It was God with such a people! From slavery to such accomplishments! Even from slavery to the Top Position of the enslavers' society! Only God could do such a thing! This People had to be God's People! This People are God's People, they are Jews, Black Jews!

Throughout the history of mankind, God has used the Jews to get his Word out to the inhabitants of the earth. This is why I could not understand two very important things. One, why God chose Williams J. Seymour? Two, why God chose me?

Before I tell you this next very important thing, let me tell you about this. Do not dismiss what I am about to say, especially if you are Black. You will see why I tell you these things. To get born again/saved is as Jesus said.

John Ch. 3, Vs. 3 & 5
"Jesus answered and said unto him, Verily, verily, I say unto thee, Except a man be born again, he cannot see the kingdom of God. Jesus answered, Verily, verily, I say unto thee, Except a man be born of water and of the Spirit, he cannot enter into the kingdom of God."

I have a reason for giving you this. You will see it. Let me finish this. Jesus says to be born again/saved that there are two parts. One, be born of the water. Two, be born of the Spirit. To be born of water means to be baptized in water. Not any baptism, but baptized in the name of Jesus. Stay with me now. To be born of the Spirit means to be born of God's Spirit. To have the Holy Ghost means you will speak in tongues. Speaking in tongues is God using your mouth to speak a language spoken somewhere on earth that you have not learned. For a deeper understanding refer to our Book "The Door Is Closing On The Last Opportunity For Immortality". Now look at why I told you this.

Now, this is why I told you the above things. For nearly (2,000) two thousand years, the world, mankind, was without salvation until the Year <u>1901.</u> This is when God gave the Holy Ghost, evidenced by speaking in tongues, to a Black Man. This Black Man was William J. Seymour. William J. Seymour, God's Servant, started a revival which spread across the earth. Very few people know this. Very, very, few Black People know this. There are now about (40) forty million people across the earth with the Holy Ghost, that speak in tongues. Why God used William J. Seymour is because this Black Man is a Black Jew.

God prophesied through my wife, Prophetess Sylvia Franklin, back in the middle of the 1990's, and said that he would use me in a similar way as he used his servant William J. Seymour. Later on Prophetess Sylvia Franklin prophesied that I would bring renewal, revival and revolution to God's Church. God said that I, Frederick E. Franklin, a Black Man, would do these things. On May 31, 2002 at 9:00 p.m. God told me that I would establish His Smyrna Church. The Smyrna Church and the Philadelphia Church are God's Churches of the Last Days that will be in the First Resurrection, the so-called Rapture. The Church of Philadelphia is the 144,000 virgin Jews that God will choose in the Last Days from the Children of Israel. The Church of Smyrna includes all other people who will be in the First Resurrection, the so-called Rapture. I did not know when God spoke these above words to me, but I know now, that I am a Jew, even a Black Jew.

God chose William J. Seymour and God chose me, Frederick E. Franklin, to get his word out to the inhabitants of the earth, because we are Jews, even Black Jews. God chose us. Like God has always done, He uses the Jews to get his word out to the people. God has now told me to write (44) forty four books to get his word to the inhabitants of earth in these last days, the end times.

Now we will address the Inferiority Issue. The idea of Black People being inferior to Whites is laughable. I will not diminish the substance of these writings by addressing this. I, therefore, will not dignify this lie by me addressing it. I will, however, say this. God said that the Ku Klux Klan and the Slave owners of the United States were and are illiterate/ignorant and abominable witchcraft workers. Refer to our Book "Words From God, By God Appearing To Us Or Just Talking To Is, For The End Times". Refer to numbers "443" through "455".

We will now address Black People as being the minority. Recently, I heard a Documentary by, Henry Louis Gates Jr., on (PBS) Public Broadcasting System. The Documentary by, Mr. Gates, was on Black People being brought from Africa by the slave traders. It was said in Mr. Gates' Documentary, that there were (35,000) thirty five thousand shipments of Slaves from Africa. He had written documentation to show this.

It was said (35,000) thirty five thousand. This is not a misprint. When I heard this, it confirmed something that I had always been saying. I had been saying, that it is nothing but a lie that the few, (39,000,000) thirty nine million, Black People in the United States are what the Government says.

When the children of Israel went into Egypt, there were only (70) seventy of them.

Exodus Ch. 1, Vs. 1-5
"Now these are the names of the children of Israel, which came into Egypt; every man and his household came with Jacob. Reuben, Simeon, Levi, and Judah, Issachar, Zebulun, and Benjamin, Dan, and Naphtali, Gad, and Asher. And all the souls that came out of the loins of Jacob were seventy souls: for Joseph was in Egypt already."

After (400) four hundred years of slavery, the population of the Jews had increased to over (3,000,000) three million. What about the number of Black People that would have increased in (400) four hundred years.

In Mr. Henry Louis Gates Jr.'s Documentary, it was said that there were (35,000) thirty five thousand shipments of Black People/Slaves from Africa. If you assume only (10%) ten percent of the total shipments came to the United States happened (400) four hundred years ago, then there would be (3500) thirty five hundred shipments by that time. If you consider that every ship had, a modest, 100 people/slaves on it, then it would mean that (350,000) three hundred fifty thousand people/slaves were brought to the United States. Mr. Gates indicated in his Documentary related to the Slave shipments, that there were over (700,000) Slaves taken to Cuba and this was twice the number of Slaves brought to the United States. This indicates that my (3500) figure is reasonable. My (100) one hundred figure on the number of Slaves per ship, takes into account those that jumped ship; that were drowned; that made it to the land of the different islands; that died on the ships.

If you assume (50%) fifty percent of the Slaves were women, then there would be (175,000) one hundred seventy five thousand baby producing Slaves. Slaves were a valuable investment to the Slave owners and they bred the women for maximum profit. They were bred like cattle, hogs or sheep. One woman could produce (10) ten to (20) twenty babies.

I have made some very modest calculations of how many Black People had to be in the United States after slavery. I have, also, made the calculations of how many Black People would have to be in the United States at this present time. I take into account these different parameters:

1. the number of slaves who jumped ship;
2. the number of slaves who died before they made it to the United States;
3. the number of slaves who were killed trying to escape in the United States;
4. only (100) one hundred slaves per ship;
5. a woman having only (5) five babies;
6. a slave only having a life span of (50) fifty years;
7. only (10%) ten percent of shipments;
8. assume it took (50) fifty years to get at (10%) ten percent of shipments.

Note this. There is no record or evidence that there were large numbers of Slaves killed trying to escape. There is no record or evidence that Slaves died because of disease. There is no record or evidence of there being any lack of Slaves for breeding. Remember, women Slaves were required to breed from (10) ten to (20) twenty babies. Some ships could carry at least (200) two hundred Slaves on it. The first shipment of Slaves came to the United States in the Year of 1619. Assume it took (50) fifty years to get at (10%) ten of shipments, then this would be around the Year of 1670.

I have made the calculations below. Follow me. Here are the calculations:

3500 shipments at 100 Slaves per ship = 350,000 Slaves

Assume half were women, = 175,000 women Slaves

After 50 years (1670-1720)—175,000 having 5 children

= 875,000 children/Slaves

Assume half were women, = 437,500 women Slaves

After 100 years (1720-1770) — 437,500 having 5 children

= 2,187,500 children/Slaves

Assume half were women, = 1,093,750 women Slaves

After 150 years (1770-1820) — 1,093,750 having 5 children

= 5,468,750 children/Slaves

Assume half are women, = 2,734,350 women Slaves

After 200 years (1820-1870) — 2,734,350 having 5 children

=13,671,750 children/Slaves

Assume half are women, = 6,835,875 women Slaves

After 250 years (1870-1920) — 6,835,875 having 5 children

= 39,179,375 children/Slaves

Assume half are women, = 19,589,688 women Slaves

After 300 years (1920-1970) — 19,589,688 having 5 children

= 97,948,440 children/Slaves

Assume half are women, = 48,974,110 women Slaves

After 350 years (1970-2020) — 48,974,110 having 5 children

= 244,870,550 children/Slaves.

After (400) four hundred years, the children of Israel who went into Egypt had increased from (70) seventy people to over (3,000,000) three million people. After (400) four years, the Slaves, Black Jews, who were shipped into the United States, and their Off Spring, increased to about (245,000,000) two hundred forty five million. After (250) two hundred fifty years of slavery, there were (39,179,375) thirty nine million, one hundred seventy thousand, three hundred seventy five Slaves, Black Jews, in the United States. This is all the

United States' Government wants to tell us that are in the United States right now.

My calculations showed that there would be (245,000,000) two hundred forty five million Black People, Black Jews, in the United States, for the women having just five children. If you consider that a Slave was required to have up to (20) twenty plus children, then the above figures that we gave should be a reasonable representation of the number of Black People in the United States. Rather than the anemic (39,000,000) thirty nine million figure that the Government says of Black People in the United States, it could actually be over (6) six times that many, (245,000,000) two forty five million Black People in the United States.

Genesis Ch. 22, V. 17
"That in blessing I will bless thee, and in multiplying I will multiply thy seed as the stars of the heaven, and as the sand which is upon the sea shore; and thy seed shall possess the gate of his enemies . . ."

Note this. Up until a few years ago, in the 1940's or 1950's, Black People were having large families. It was a common thing, average size, for a family to have about (10) ten children in a family. So you can see that family size has tended to decrease as the time approaches the now/present. So, you can see that the (5) five member family used in my calculation is a modest figure. When

I was growing up, as a child, one of my friend's mother had (21) twenty one healthy Black children, including himself. My Grandmother, Selena Tolbert, had (13) thirteen children. My Grandfather's and Grandmother's daughter Edna, my mother, had (12) twelve brothers and sisters. Ervin, Clarence, (Bishop) Pearlie, Curtis, Eski Luvern, Freda, Rufus, LeGrant, Verna, Joyce Voncile, Erma Jean and Nadene. My wife's, Prophetess Sylvia Franklin's, mother, Annie Mae Flowers, had (10) ten brothers and sisters. On my wife's father side of her family, her father was a part of a family of ten brothers and sisters. My wife is much younger than I am. So you can see the gradual decrease in family size. Thirteen (13) children from my mother's family to (10) ten children from my wife's mother's and father's family. Excuse the diversion, let us get back on course.

If you think that the (245,000,000) two hundred five figure that I determine is too high, consider this. When the Slaves, the Jews, were in Egypt of old, the Slaves, the Jews, increased to the level of out—numbering the Egyptians.

Exodus Ch. 1, Vs. 8 & 9
"Now there arose up a new king over Egypt, which new not Joseph. And he said unto his people, Behold, the people of the children of Israel are more and mightier than we."

The United States being the modern day Egypt, then the Black People, Black Jews, would out-number the White People. This makes very good sense when you consider that White People were not having large families.

Revelation Ch. 11, V. 8

". . . the great city, which spiritually is called Sodom and Egypt . . ."

Even if we consider more modest parameters, the population of Black People, Black Jews, in the United States is greater than that anemic (39,000,000) thirty nine million figure that the Government says. We know, from the records and the encyclopedia, that slavery in the United States was at its height around 1793. This is when the cotton gin was invented and utilized. If we consider the following parameters for our calculations:

1. start at the Year of 1800;
2. use again only 10% shipments of Slaves by that time;
3. a (50) fifty year life span for the Slaves;
4. shipments of only 100 Slaves per ship;
5. use a family size of (10) ten children for the first (150) one hundred fifty years;
6. use a family size of (5) five children for the last (50) fifty years;
7. use only (200) two hundred years of Black People being in the United States.

With these very modest parameters, we yet get a much higher population for Black People, Black Jews, in the United States than the Government says. The following are my calculations:

10% of 35000 shipments = 3500

3500 shipments of 100 Slaves per ship = 350,000

Assume half are women, = 175,000 women Slaves

175,000 having 10 children = 1,750,000, 750,000 Slaves/ Black Jews after 50 years (1800-1850)

Assume half are women, = 875,000 women Slaves

875,000 having 10 children = 8,750,000

8,750,000 Slaves/Black Jews after 100 years (1850-1900)

Assume half are women, = 4,375,000 women Slaves

4,375,000 having 10 children = 43,750,000

43,750,000 Slaves/Black Jews after 150 years (1900-1950)

Assume half are women, = 21,875,000 women Slaves

21,875,000 having 5 children = 109,375,000

109,375,000 Slaves/Black Jews after 200 years (1950-2000)

By the Year of 2000 there would have been at least (109,375,000) one hundred nine million, three hundred seventy five thousand Black People, Black Jews, in the United States. That is a far cry from (39,000,000) thirty nine million. This (109,375,000) one hundred nine million, three hundred seventy five thousand figure did not consider it being any Slaves in the United States before the Year of 1800. The first shipment of Slaves came into the United States in 1619. Also, women were bred to have up to (20) twenty children; sometimes even more. So we know that the population figure could not be less than that (109,375,000) one hundred nine million, three hundred seventy five thousand figure. There is no way for Black People, Black Jews, to be a minority in the United States. If those Slaves had only known that they were not a minority. This is why so many White folks are obsessed with guns. This is why the (NRA) National Rifle Association is like unto their God. This is why they were/are convinced that President Barack Obama would do away with their guns. Rather than being against the idea of President Barack Obama taking away guns from the population, they should be for him taking them away. Think, a Black People in the majority having guns who you enslaved. If the Black

People, Black Jews, was as salvage as they, some White folks, claim us to be, then these White folks, contrary to what they are doing, should be promoting gun control. Thank God we are not the salvage beast that they say we are. We have not enslaved a people.

Matthew Ch. 18, V. 7
"Woe unto the world because of offenses: for it must needs be that offenses come; but woe that man by whom the offense cometh."

Genesis Ch. 12, V. 3
"And I will bless them that bless thee, and curse him that curseth thee . . ."

The number of Black People in the United States has been the top of the top of secrets in the United States. I do not believe that even the Black President Barack Obama knows this secret. The White Slave owners of the United States wanted the Slaves to think that there were only a few of us to keep us under control, mind control witchcraft.

When the Jews were Slaves in Egypt and they began to increase, Egypt became afraid. Egypt said that the Jews would out-number the Egyptians and they were afraid that the Jews would rise up against them.

<u>Exodus Ch. 1, Vs. 6-10</u>

"And Joseph died, and all his brethren, and all that generation. And the children of Israel were fruitful, and increase abundantly, and multiplied, and waxed exceeding mighty; and the land was filled with them. Now there arose up a new king over Egypt, which knew not Joseph. And he said unto his people, Behold, the people of the children of Israel are more and mightier than we: Come on, let us deal wisely with them; lest they multiply, and it come to pass, that, when there falleth out any war, they join also unto our enemies, and fight against us, and so get them up out of the land. Therefore they did set over them taskmasters to afflict them with their burdens . . . But the more they afflicted them, the more they multiplied and grew. And they were grieved because of the children of Israel. And the Egyptians made the children of Israel to serve with rigour: And they made their lives bitter with hard bondage, in morter, and in brick, and in all manner of service in the field: all their service, wherein they made them serve, was with rigour."

To control the situation in Egypt, the king ordered the midwives to kill all of the male babies to limit the Jews population.

<u>Exodus Ch. 1, V. 15</u>

"And the king of Egypt spake to the Hebrew midwives . . . And he said, When ye do the office of a midwife to the Hebrew women, and see them upon the stools; if it be a son, then ye shall kill him: but if it be a daughter, then she shall live."

After slavery in the United States, the way that the United States tried to control the Black People's, Black Jews', population was/is to:

1. make us so destitute that we would destroy ourselves;
2. try to starve us out by not letting us get a job;
3. get dope in the Black communities;
4. develop a prison system mainly for Black People;
5. use the syphilis experiment at the Tuskegee's VA Hospital to inject the infectious disease in the Black community;
6. require that Black People have degrees to get a job;
7. etc.

In an effort in the South of the United States to make us destitute and to starve us out, was to require that we have a college degree to get a decent job. White folks did not have to have a college degree. They were not even required to have a high school diploma. This education requirement discrimination has tended to backfire on the White folks. It has resulted in a large number of Black Jews being educated and large number of the White population being uneducated. A few years ago, even the Governor of the State of Alabama did not have a college degree; Governor Guy Hunt. This college degree requirement was part of a designed larger scheme to take the Black People's land. What would happen is that a Black man would be given a minimum paying job. Then they, the Whites, would convince that Black person to send their child or children to college to get a degree so the child or children could get a better job. You might say, that sounds very noble of them. Let me finish. Well, they, the Whites, knew that the Black family had no money for college. So the White folks convince them of the security of their job and further convinced them to take out a loan with the local bank. Well, their job was not sufficient for the loan. Well, the banker and the employer would then convince the Black family to put its land up for collateral. Once the transaction was completed, the Black person would be fired from his/her job. Usually, the banker and the employer were close relatives. Also, the other employers in the area would be relatives or friends. They all would be co-conspirators of the same lodge/order of the terrorist (KKK) Ku Klux Klan. The Black person now having no job and no way of getting a job and therefore had no money, would therefore default on the loan and therefore would lose their land. Black People who had land and many did, would be targeted for this scheme. This scheme was repeated over and over again down south. A very devious scheme collaborated with the employers, bankers and even governments; all of them being co-conspirators of the terrorist (KKK) Ku Klux Klan. You might ask, how do I know all of these things? I am an Apostle of God.

Matthew Ch. 10, V. 26

". . . for there is nothing covered, that shall not be revealed; and hid, that shall not be known."

When the education scheme would not work, the White folks would just take the land. I know of an instance in South Alabama where a Black man owned several hundred acres of land. A certain White man wanted his land. So the White man paid taxes on his land, even though the Black man had paid his taxes on the land. The White man then went to court for the Black man to be evicted from his land. The judge ruled that the Black man had to relinquish his land, but the White man had to pay him for the tax money he had paid when they paid the taxes at the same time.

When the White folks could not take the land through the courts with this tax scheme, they would forge the documents to get ownership of the Black People's land. I have personal and direct knowledge of such. My grandfather had this done to him. My grandfather was a visionary. He came to Mobile, Alabama of the United States many years ago. The County of Mobile was mainly swamp and forest at that time. My grandfather was a man of wealth and great wisdom. He used his money to buy up the swamp and wooded area in south Mobile County that no one wanted. Land at that time only was considered good if it was cleared and you could farm on it. So the swamp and wooded land was very cheap. My grandfather saw what could be. Well, my grandfather bought up all this cheap land that he could get, over (2000) two thousand acres. My grandfather would buy this land, then clear it for farming. As wise as my grandfather was, he had a very unwise habit, he was known to keep all of his important papers, including deeds to his land, on him. Some White folks along with some Black co-conspirators, planned a scheme to steal my grandfather's deeds and to forge them. While clearing his land in a place called Dawes in southwest Mobile, they killed my grandfather and stole his deeds. Those White devils and uncle Tom Black devils blew my grandfather up with the dynamite that he was using to clear his land. They, the White devils and uncle Tom devils, the co-conspirators, took his deeds and forged their names on the deeds. The Black men in this conspiracy were given a small token of this land for their help. My grandfather's name is HENRY NEAL TOLBERT. MY GRANDFATHER'S GENEOLOGY LEADS TO THE TOLBERT SUB-TRIBE IN AFRICA, WHICH I BELIEVE WAS OF THE TRIBE OF JUDAH.

God allowed me to give my grandfather's testimony in this book for a token of his love for me.

Matthew Ch. 10, V. 26

". . . for there is nothing covered, that shall not be revealed; and hid, that shall not be known."

In the slavery years, there arose up in the United States a certain group of evil people called Mormons. This group is the twin of the terrorist (KKK) Ku Klux Klan. This group has come up with its own lying religion. This group espouses:

1. that JESUS has a half-brother who is Lucifer/ Satan;

2. that the angels that were kicked out of heaven by GOD +was Lucifer and the other Black angels;

3. that there would be no Civil War in the United States;

4. that Black People would always be the slaves of White People in the United States;

5. that they could get anyone into heaven who they wanted to, no matter how bad they lived their lives, even Adolph Hitler;

6. that they could get anyone into heaven by simply one of their members being baptized for them when they were dead;

7. that the blood of JESUS CHRIST is not sufficient to Atone for all sins;

8. that your own blood must be shed to Atone for some sins;

9. that they do not believe that the King James Version of the Holy Scriptures/Bible is totally true;

10. (other lies).

The group that espouses the above things is called the Mormons. One of the leading Republican candidates for the Presidency is a member of the Mormons' Church, Mitt Romney. This Mormons' Church is also called The Church Of Jesus Christ Of Latter-Day Saints. Is it not an irony to have the name "Jesus Christ" in your Church's name and believe the above things. Mitt Romney has been a long time pastor in this religion. He, also, says that he believes the things above and will never change his mind about them. So much for the Republican Party espousing that it is the Party of the Christians. You Hypocrites! For them hating a Black Man is above them loving GOD. GOD said that there will never be another Republican President. As a side issue, let me prophesy this. The scheming of the Republicans to limit the people to vote who would vote for President Barack Obama, will backfire on them. They condemned themselves with their scheming. In the States of this scheming, God's judgment will be upon you because of the evil behind your scheming.

I could tell you of your judgment, but I will not at this time.

<u>Psalm 75, Vs. 6 & 7</u>
"For promotion cometh neither from the east, nor from the west, nor from the south. But God is the judge: he putteth down one, and setteth up another."

In recent years, the United States (the terrorist KKK and its evil co-espousers) have not so much been concerned with the Black People rising up against it in war, but, rather, by them getting control and power through the vote. We have used the name (KKK) Ku Klux Klan in representing the evil of the United States, however, it also represents all of the White supremacy espousers of the United States; including: Nazi groups, militia groups, skin heads, etc. One day a few years ago, as I drove up into a parking lot at a local grocery store in Mobile, Alabama, God spoke to me. God said that the reason that the (KKK) Ku Klux Klan is against abortion, is because of the vote. God said that they are worried and afraid of Black People winning elections. They are worried and afraid of being in the minority. God said that the KKK knows that White women have more abortions than other women. The percentage of White women having abortions far exceeds all other women combined. God said that the Ku Klux Klan would not care if Black babies and other non-White babies are aborted. I had always wondered why as evil as the terrorist Ku Klux Klan is, why could it be right concerning abortions. For abortion is indeed the murder of babies. Well, God let me know why.

What we have seen are the ways that the United States have tried to control the Black People, the Black Jews. God said that the truth would set us free.

John Ch. 8, V. 32
"And ye shall know the truth and the truth shall make you free."

As Black People, as Black Jews, this book sets us free of the lie, the mind control witchcraft, that we are illiterate. Well, we already knew better than that. As Black People, as Black Jews, this book sets us free of the lie, the mind control witchcraft, that we have no important heritage. As Black People, as Black Jews, this book sets us free of the lie, the mind control witchcraft, that we are inferior to White People. Well, we did not need the book to let us know that. As Black People, Black Jews, this book sets us free of the lie, of the mind control witchcraft, that we are in the minority. This book should make us free to receive the truth of what God said in the Holy Scriptures/Bible, so we can be saved.

Romans Ch. 11, V. 24
"For if thou wert cut out of the tree which is wild by nature, and wert grafted contrary to nature into a good

146

olive tree: how much more shall these, which be natural branches, be grafted into their own olive tree."

No longer will we have to believe the same religion as our slave owners. It is amazing that we could think/believe that the same religion of our slave owners could be right. AMAZING! ABSOLUTELY AMAZING! So influencing, so encompassing, so complete, so effective, has been their mind control witchcraft against us. How could we believe that their perverted rendering of the Scriptures of the Holy Bible could be true? How could we believe that the perverted rendering of the Scriptures of the Holy Bible by the terrorist Ku Klux Klan could be true? How could we believe what they said about us are who we are? So great has been their divination, their sorcery, their wizardry, against us. The Grand Wizard is the Title of the Head of the terrorist (KKK) Ku Klux Klan. The terrorist Ku Klux Klan and the Slave owners are the same. They used/use the same wizardry to control the Black People, Black Jews. There perverted interpretation of the Scriptures are what we have believed. We have even had Black Preachers to try to validate their perverted interpretations of the Scriptures to us. They all, nearly all, (99%) ninety nine percent of them, said and say, the same thing as Billy Graham said/say. They all said/say the same thing as Paul Crouch said/say. They all said/say the same thing as the non-Jew terrorist (KKK) Ku Klux Klan. The

Catholic Church is even worse in its lies than those so-called Protestant Churches. Refer to our Books:

1. "Proof That Your Leaders Have Deceived You And The End Times"
2. "The Name Of The (Anti-Christ) Beast And 666 Identification"
3. "The Door Is Closing On The Last Opportunity For Immortality"

Let me show you another similarity of God's people, the Black Jews, in the United States and Egypt of old. In Egypt of old, the children of Israel were in captivity there for (400) four hundred years. After (400) four hundred years in bondage, Moses delivered the children of Israel out of bondage. I have said that this book will set Black People, Black Jews, in the United States free. From 1619 to the time of publication of this book is (400) four hundred years. From the time, Year of 1619, to the Year of 2012 is (400) four hundred years. You might say, that is not (400) four hundred years. I say, yes it is. A year according to God is 360 days. Refer to the following Scriptures:

1. Revelation Ch. 13, V. 5
2. Revelation Ch. 11, Vs. 2 & 3
3. Revelation Ch. 12, Vs. 6 & 14
4. Daniel Ch. 7, V. 25

Man says that a year is 365 days or 366 days for a leap year. If we believe God, there are 360 days in a year. This means that from 1619 to 2012 there are (400) four hundred years. This is an easy calculation to make. This book's publication date is 2012.

I have never written of this before, what I am about to tell you. Not in all of our previous (43) four three books. I do not tell you this to boast. God hates pride and so do I. I tell you this that you might believe these writings, so that you might be saved. In the Year of 1995, while living Montgomery, Alabama, while sitting on my bed, God spoke to me and said that I am like Moses. About a day or two after God told me this, my son, Elijah Jeremiah Ezekiel Franklin, a few days after he had been filled with the Holy Ghost, evidenced by speaking in tongues, said that God said to him, that I am like Moses. My son was filled with the Holy Ghost at five years old. Moses led the children of Israel out of the bondage of Egypt and God is using me to lead his People, the Black Jews, out of the bondage of the spiritual Egypt, the United States. A few days after my son said God told him I am like Moses, a brother and a prophet who lived in Montgomery, came by our house and said that God told him to go and tell me that I am like Moses.

One of the tricks of the terrorist (KKK) Ku Klux Klan was to get us to accept their interpretation of the Scriptures so they could use them against us. Two of the main

Scriptures they used were the Scriptures on forgiveness and turning the other cheek. In their thinking, if they could get us to buy into their interpretation of these Scriptures, then they would not have to worry about the Blacks after slavery rising up against them.

You might say, piously and religiously, the Scriptures of the Holy Bible do indeed say that you must forgive and turn the other cheek. I say unto you, the Scriptures indeed say these things, but your teachers and your interpretation of these Scriptures are not what you have been taught. You can find words in the Bible to say anything that you want. You can find words in the Bible that indicate that God is a liar. We know that this is not true. You might say, wait a minute, wait a minute, you are blaspheming. No I am not. Then you might say, show it to me, show me that Scripture, if you can; I know that it is not in my Bible that I read, you might say. Well, will the King James Version be alright? Look at I Corinthians Chapter 13.

I Corinthians Ch. 13, V. 7
"Beareth all things, believeth all things, hopeth all things, endureth all things."

You could say, according to the above Scripture, that God is a liar because you believe that he is a liar. You might say, I believe that Satan is as powerful as his creator GOD. Well, we know that this is a gross lie too. Satan is nothing. His only claim to status is that he can deceive some of mankind that he is something. So you can see that without proper interpretation of the Scriptures, you can be in error.

The Holy Scriptures of the Bible also talks about Restitution. Why you never hear about this preaching from White folks. Let us get back to forgiveness and turning the other cheek. When the Holy Scriptures of the Bible were written, they were written as a will to God's People. That is what the Old Testament and New Testament are, they are wills. When Jesus was talking about turning the other cheek, he was talking about turning the other the cheek to your brother or sister. Your brother or sister is one who is born again/saved.

Matthew Ch. 5, V. 39
". . . but whosoever shall smite thee on thy right cheek, turn to him the other also."

You can see that this Scripture is only referring to God's People by reading the previous Scripture. When it says an eye for eye and a tooth for a tooth. This was what Moses gave/said to the children of Israel in the Law.

Matthew Ch. 5, V. 38
"Ye have heard that it hath been said, An eye for an eye, and a tooth for a tooth . . ."

Exodus Ch. 21, Vs. 23 & 24

"And if any mischief follow, then thou shalt give life for life, Eye for eye, tooth for tooth, hand for hand, foot for foot . . ."

This is what God told his people to be toward each other. What about their enemies? God killed them or he had the children of Israel, his People, to kill them. We, God's People, do not kill in this day and time under the New Covenant, but God yet kills his People's enemies.

Let us get back to the main point. Turning the other cheek as Jesus said, means turning the other cheek to your brother or sister. Your brother and sister are those who are born of the Spirit. If you speak in tongues you are born of the Spirit, but if you do not get baptized in the name of Jesus, you will go to hell. Now you can see why the lie on salvation has been so pushed by Satan and the terrorist (KKK) Ku Klux Klan. They want you to think that if you just say that you believe in Jesus, then you are born again/saved. Therefore if they burn your house down, you were not or are not, to do anything about it. If they beat you, you were not supposed or are not suppose, to do anything about it. If they took your land, you were not supposed or are not suppose, to do anything about it. Even if they killed your family members, you were supposed or are not suppose, to do anything about it. To get a better understanding, we suggest that you read our Books:

1. "The Door Is Closing On The Last Opportunity For Immortality"
2. "Words From God, By God Appearing To Us Or Just Talking To Us, For The End Times"

You might say, the Scriptures also said you had to forgive. The Scriptures never told us to forgive automatically. To always or automatically forgive is another one of their lying interpretations. Here again the Scriptures are telling a brother or sister to forgive another brother or sister. There is no contradiction in God's word. God said that forgiveness was required for a brother or sister if they asked for forgiveness. Not only should he or she ask for forgiveness, but also he or she must be sincere. The brother or sister must be repented, then you are required to forgive.

<u>Luke Ch. 17, V. 3</u>
"Take heed to yourselves: If thy brother trespass against thee, rebuke; and if he repent, forgive him."

We have been taught by some ignorant and evil White folks and our ignorant Black preachers to just forgive no matter what.

You might ask, what about the non-violent effort of the civil rights era, it told us to turn the other cheek and to forgive and it worked. No! No! No! The history of the so-called civil rights era is a lie. History is nothing but a White man's lie. The change came to this country by God. God did it in spite of the non-violent proponents. During the time of the so-called civil rights era, the United States changed only because of the competition between the United States and the former (USSR) Union of Soviet Socialist Republic for Africa's natural resources of oil, diamonds, silver gold, etc. There was competition between Capitalism and Communism to win the nations and countries of the world. There was growing influence during that time by the Black Panthers, Black Muslims, Malcolm X, Rap Brown and others. On the other side were the non-violent espousers. God caused these efforts of these two sides to be heard all over the earth, including in Africa. Africa's Black population was of course sympathetic to the struggle. The USSR saw an opportunity to exploit the situation to gain a foothold in Africa. So, the USSR announced that it was on the side of the Black People's struggle in the United States.

God put it in the mind of the Leader of the USSR, Nikita Khrushchev, to take advantage of this Black struggle for equality in the United States.

Proverbs Ch. 21, V. 1
"THE king's heart is in the hand of the LORD, as the rivers of water: he turneth it whithersoever he will."

The United States realized why the USSR and Nikita Khrushchev were saying that they were on the side of the Black People struggle for equality and began to make some modest change. It all had to do with Africa and its natural resources.

Since the United States recognized that it had to change, it chose to build up the non-violent effort over the militant other side. After all the terrorist (KKK) Ku Klux Klan could not have dreamed of a better situation for them than that which was espoused by the non-violent side.

It is the time for truth to be revealed. It is time for God's word to be fulfilled.

<u>Matthew Ch. 10, V. 26</u>
". . . for there is nothing covered, that shall not be revealed; and hid, that shall not be known."

Now I, a Black Jew, say that their religions are wrong and are not what God said in the Holy Scriptures/Bible. My credentials of being God's servant, even an Apostle, are substantial. Will you believe me, a Black Jew, a person who has heritage with Jesus Christ or will you believe the Slave owners and the terrorist (KKK) Ku Klux Klan. Jesus said that in the last days that this perversion would be believed on this earth. Jesus said that people would be deceived. To deceive, Satan tells you some small obvious truth to get you to believe a larger lie.

<u>Matthew Ch. 24, V. 5</u>
"For many shall come in my name, saying, I am Christ; and shall deceive many."

When I live in Montgomery, Alabama, as I walk into my kitchen, God spoke to me and said that I had been cautious to make sure that I would not be deceived by the anti-Christ, the man, but I am already in that time. God let me know that the above Scripture of Matthew Chapter 24, Verse 5, is referring to the many so-called Christian Churches. All of them say that Jesus is Christ, the son of God, but they all are deceiving many. God let me know that they are deceiving the people on salvation. God, also, said that they are deceiving the people saying, that we will not have to go through the period known as the Great Tribulation. Refer to our Books:

1. "The Door Is Closing On The Last Opportunity For Immortality"
2. "Words From God, By God Appearing To Us Or Just Talking To Us, For The End Time"

All of these so-called Christian Churches are saying that Jesus could come back at any time and that we will not have to endure the troubles of the Book of Revelation. This is a lie. Refer to our Books:

1. "The Judgment Of The United States"
2. "Proof That Your Leaders Have Deceived You And The End Times"
3. "Words From God, By God Appearing To Us Or Just Talking To Us, For The End Times"
4. "Five Month Desire To Die, But Not Possible When Fifth Angel Blows Trumpet"
5. "The Name Of The (Anti-Christ) Beast And 666 Identification"
6. "The Door Is Closing On The Last Opportunity For Immortality"

Jesus coming at any minute or any day is a lie. However, if you die, it makes no difference. You will go to hell if you are not born again/saved. Black People, Black Jews, and others, I suggest, I recommend, I urge, you to get born again/saved, as we have told you. I urge you to do as the Black Jews' kindred JESUS CHRIST has said; be born of water and the Spirit; so you can be in the First Resurrection, the so-called Rapture; so you can go to be with God; that your soul will not burn in hell and the lake of fire.

If you are a Black Jew, wouldn't it be a shame, to find out after all of these years, that you have heritage with Jesus, but yet end up going to hell because you did not obey him. Black Jews, non-Black Jews and non-Jews, hear my plea. Obey Jesus Christ the Jew, the Son of God, God that was on the earth among mankind in the flesh.

We the Black People of the United States will not rise up in violence against White People, for we are God's People, the Black Jews. We do not have the nature of the Barbaric and Savage. We have no desire to kill another human being as you in your Savagery have taught us. We have no right, nor desire, to destroy a vessel of creation of the ALMIGHTY GOD.

Just as in the past, with the children of God, the children of Israel, we will not rise up against Egypt. Yet we will not be enslaved again as some of you desire. I prophesy to you and against you. We, the Black People, the Black Jews, will not recompense you for your evil. Yet, you will be recompensed. GOD WILL DO IT, EVEN AS HE DID IN EGYPT OF OLD. They saw the boils on their bodies. There, however, were no boils on God's People. They had their water polluted with blood. There, however, was pure and fresh water for God's People. They saw the pestilence of flies and frogs upon them and their properties and possessions. There, however, were not the same with God's People. As the wrath of God came upon Egypt of Old, so will it come upon the enemies of his People of the United States.

God will cause the likeness with the White folks who are the enemies of his People in the United States.

I prophesy, yet again as an Apostle of God. God will recompense the modern day Egypt, the United States. Through tornadoes and other weather conditions and others, God will recompense you. YOU WILL KNOW THAT IT IS FROM GOD. God prophesied through my wife, Prophetess Sylvia Franklin, a few years ago and said that something bad is going to start happening to White folks. I further prophesy, there will be great death and great morning among you. There will be great fires among you and cause great destruction and death. A Great Depression will result from the continual turmoil. Your insurance companies will fail because of the constant problems, plagues and destruction.

For those of you who will not hear our words, including the Black Jews, a Great Plague will come on this earth upon all of you, young and old, great and small, rich and poor, moral and ungodly. This will happen to all who do not speak in tongues. You will want to die, but you will not be able to die. This plague will cause excruciating pain. This plague will last for five months. After this, there will be a Great War on this earth that will cause (1/3) one third of the people on earth to be killed. During these times, President Barack Obama will be removed from the Presidency by the (Anti-Christ) Beast, Pope John Paul II (Carol Josef Wojtyla) and former President Bill Clinton. President Barack Obama will be killed by them (15) fifteen months after he is removed from office. Even before this Great War, there will be at least (2) two other very significant wars on this earth. After this Great War, the 666 Great Tribulation period will start. Immediately following this, the First Resurrection, the so-called Rapture, will occur. Immediately following this, the Wrath of God will be poured out on this earth ending with the Battle of Armageddon. Refer to our Books:

1. "Five Month Desire To Die, But Not Possible When Fifth Angel Blows Trumpet"
2. "The Name Of The (Anti-Christ) Beast And 666 Identification"
3. "The Door Is Closing On The Last Opportunity For Immortality"
4. "Words From God, By God Appearing To Us Or Just Talking To Us, For The End Times"

This is a late insertion to the book. GOD gave me some added revelation for the book. The terrorist (KKK) Ku Klux Klan and its co-espousers have been taught about the End Times by the so-called prophecy teachers of this day. They all have been saying, correctly, that the so-called anti-Christ will have to be a Jew. They have been fervently preaching this for years. They have correctly been basing their assertion on the Scripture of Daniel Chapter 11.

Daniel Ch. 11, Vs. 36 & 37

"And the king shall do according to his will; and he shall exalt himself above every god, and shall speak marvelous things against the God of gods, and shall prosper till the indignation be accomplished: for that that is determined shall be done. Neither shall he regard the God of his fathers, nor the desire of women, nor regard any god: for he shall magnify himself above all."

The phrase in the above Scripture which says "the God of his fathers" indicates that he is a Jew. The so-called anti-Christ will have a Jewish heritage.

When President Barack Obama became President, all of the so-called prophecy teachers declared, incorrectly, that President Barack Obama was the so-called anti-Christ. GOD told me on Thursday, April 5, 2012, that them knowing that Black People are Jews, is why they say that President Barack Obama is the so-called anti-Christ. They have known all the time that Black People are Jews, but they did not want to let us know that we are Jews. SO SAYS GOD. President Barack Obama being a Jew is how the real (anti-Christ) Beast, Pope John Paul II, Carol Josef Wojtyla and former President Bill Clinton can pull off the deception that President Barack Obama is the anti-Christ. SO SAYS GOD. Refer to our Books:

1. "The Name Of The (Anti-Christ) Beast And 666 Identification"
2. "Words From God, By God Appearing To Us Or Just Talking To Us, For The End Times

CHAPTER 3

<u>Back To Africa</u>

(THE FINAL EXODUS)

Before we get into the main subject, let us give you a quick summary of what will happen on this earth in the future. We are now in the beginning of sorrows time. Refer to Matthew Chapter 24.

<u>Matthew Ch. 24, Vs. 4-8</u>
"And Jesus answered and said unto them, Take heed that no man deceive you. For many shall come in my name, saying, I am Christ; and shall deceive many. And ye shall hear of wars and rumours of wars: see that ye be not trouble: for all these things must come to pass, but the end is not yet. For nation shall rise against nation, and kingdom against kingdom: and there shall be famines, and pestilences, and earthquakes in divers places. All these are the beginning sorrows."

God spoke to my wife, Prophetess Sylvia Franklin, a few years ago, and said that we are in <u>the beginning of sorrows time.</u>

After <u>the beginning of sorrows time,</u> their will be <u>the great tribulation.</u> After the great tribulation, will be <u>the</u>

First Resurrection, the so-called rapture. After the First Resurrection, will be the wrath of God. The wrath of God includes the Battle of Armaggedon. The Battle of Armaggedon ends the wrath of God. After the Battle of Armaggedon, will be the millennium period, the (1000) one thousand years. After the millennium period, will be the white throne judgment. The white throne judgment is the very end. God has not told Mankind anything past the white throne judgment.

Now let us get into the main subject. God told us that only (148,000) one hundred forty eight thousand souls will be saved in the United States. This was first of all shocking! Shocking because at that time, there was nearly (300,000,000) three hundred million people living in the United States! Not only that, but the United States is the so-called Christian Nation. So much for that lie. Now, at this time, it is (300,000,000) million people in the United States. Only (148,000) one hundred forty eight thousand souls being saved, being in the First Resurrection, the so-called rapture, however, this seems that very many of God's people, the Jews, Black and non-Black, would be lost. This was a hard pill to swallow! As we showed in Chapter 2 of this Book, there are around (200,000,000) two hundred million Black and non-Black Jews in the United States; then, this means that nearly all of them would be lost. This was very frustrating to us; because we knew if God said it, it will be so; only (148,000) one hundred forty eight thousand will be saved in the United States.

God has said that in these last days, the end times, it will be like in the days of Noah and as the days of Sodom. God, also, said that the United States will be like Egypt of old; God, also, said that the United States, however, was like Sodom. In Chapter 1 and Chapter 2 of this Book we showed these things.

Luke Ch. 17, Vs. 26,28 & 30
"And as it was in the days of Noe, so shall it be also in the days of the Son of man. Likewise also as it was in the days of Lot. Even thus shall it be in the days when the Son of man is revealed."

In the above Scriptures, Noe is the same as Noah. Well, in the days of Noah and in the days of Sodom, only a few were saved. Only eight were saved in Noah's day and only three were saved when Sodom was destroyed. Noah, his wife, three sons and their wives were saved in Noah's day. When Sodom was destroyed, only Lot and his two daughters were saved.

Genesis Ch. 7, Vs. 1,4 & 7
"And the LORD said unto Noah, Come thou and all thy house into the ark; for thee have I seen righteous before me in this generation. For in seven days, and I will cause it to rain upon the earth forty days and forty

nights; and every living substance will I destroy from off the face of the earth. And his sons, and his wife, and his son's wives with him, into the ark, because of the floods."

Before we go any further let us point this out. We are straying somewhat from the main subject, but let us mention this. As we mentioned in Chapter 1, Satan has two of his ministers who have a television program, belching out lies across the earth, more than any of Satan's lying so-called Christian preachers. They say that not only did Noah, his wife, his son's and their wives saved in the ark, but also two of every ethnic group/race on the earth, including those of Cain's family. Well, the above Scripture of Genesis Chapter 7, Verse 1, proves this not to be true. The Scripture says, that the reason that Noah and his family was saved, was because Noah was righteous. Therefore, Cain's family and the others were not saved.

Genesis Ch. 7, V. 1
"and all thy house into the ark; for thee have I seen righteous before me in this generation"

Genesis Ch. 6, Vs. 5-7
"And God saw that the wickedness of man was very great in the earth, and every imagination of his the thoughts of his heart was only evil continually. And it repented the LORD that he had made man on the earth,

it grieved him at his heart. And the LORD said, I will destroy man whom I have created from the face of the earth; both man, and beast . . ."

Genesis Ch. 4, Vs. 13 & 14

"And Cain said unto the LORD, My punishment is greater than I can bear. Behold, thou hast driven me out this day from the face of the earth; and from thy face shall I be hid; and I shall be a fugitive and vagabond in the earth . . ."

Noah was the only righteous during that time. So, only Noah and his family was saved in the ark.

Now let us get back to the main point; about Noah and Sodom; about the few that were saved.

Genesis Ch. 19, Vs. 1,5,13,15,17, & 26

"And there came two angels to Sodom . . . And they called unto Lot, and said unto him . . . For we will destroy this place . . . And when the morning arose, then the angels hastened Lot, saying, Arise, take thy wife, and thy two daughters . . . And it came to pass, when they had brought them forth abroad, that he said, Escape for thy life; look not behind thee, neither stay thou thee in all thy plain; escape to the mountain, less thou be consumed. But his wife looked back from behind him, and she became a pillar of salt."

So, we see that only a few were saved in Noah's day and when Sodom was destroyed; however, in Egypt of old, which represented the United States, all of God's people left from it. But, God said that only (148,000) one hundred forty eight thousand would be saved; be in the First Resurrection, the so-called rapture, in the United States.

On June 12, 2013, God gave me an answer to the seemingly contradiction; only (148,000) one hundred forty eight thousand being saved in the First Resurrection and all or nearly all of God's people being delivered from Egypt of old. I received confirmation of this on June 13, 2013.

God has said in his word, that in the last days, end times, that he would call his people, the Jews, from all the nations/countries where he had scattered them. He would call them into their own land.

Ezekiel Ch. 34, Vs. 11 & 13
"For thus said the LORD God . . . so will I seek out my sheep, and delivered them out of all places where they have been scattered in the cloudy and dark day. And I will bring them out from the people, and gather them from the countries, and will bring them to their own land . . ."

Ezekiel Ch. 36, V. 24

"For I will take you from among the heathens, and gather you out of all countries, and will bring you into your own land."

Ezekiel Ch. 37, V. 14

"And shall put my Spirit in you, and ye shall live, and I will place you in your own land: then shall ye know that the LORD have spoken it, and performed it, saith the LORD."

Ezekiel Ch. 39, Vs. 25-28

"Therefore thus saith the LORD God; Now will I bring again the captivity of Jacob, and have mercy upon the whole house of Israel, and will be jealous for my holy name; After that they have borne their shame, and all their trespasses whereby they have trespassed against me, when they dwelt safely in their land, and none made them afraid. When I have brought them again from the people, and gathered them out of their enemies' land, and am sanctified in them in the sight of many nations; Then shall they know that I am the LORD their God, which cause them to be led into captivity among the heathen: but I have gathered them into their own land, and have left none of them any more there."

So we see that God will bring his people from the lands/ countries where they were taken captivity. This surely would include Black people of the United States. So,

God wants his people to leave the United States. Leave the United States, the spiritual Egypt, as God brought his people out of the Egypt of old. There will be some few that will be here in the United States of God's people by the time that the First Resurrection, the so-called rapture, takes place; they, however, will be dead. All, as the above Scripture indicates, will leave the United States in the Great Exodus. This Great Exodus will take place before the First Resurrection, the so-called rapture. God has let us know that the United States will be totally destroyed immediately after the First Resurrection, the so-called rapture takes place. Pope John Paul II, Carol Josef Wojtyla, the (Anti-Christ) Beast and Former President Bill Clinton, the other Beast, False Prophet, will have the United States destroyed. They will have it destroyed to shut the voice up of the few saints in the United States who will be exposing/revealing them, the (Anti-Christ) and the False Prophet, for who they are. Refer to our Books:

1. "The Name Of The (Anti-Christ) Beast And 666 Identification"
2. "Who Is The (False Prophet) Second Beast"
3. "United States In The Bible"
4. "The Judgment Of The United States"
5. "The Ten Horns Of The Books Of Daniel And Revelation"
6. "Words From God, By God Talking To Us Or Just Talking To Us, For The End Times"

God clearly shows that he calls his people out of the United States in the Book of Revelation of the New Testament of the Holy Scriptures/Bible.

<u>Revelation Ch. 18, V. 4</u>

"And I heard another voice from heaven saying, Come out of her, my people, that ye be not partakers of her sins, and ye receive not of her plagues."

Therefore, a Great Exodus will take place from the United States of God's people; especially those who were taken captive. Well, we know the only ones who were taken into captivity here in the United States were the Black Jews.

The idea of leaving the United States is absolutely insane to most who live in the United States. Since Black people, Black Jews, makeup such a large part of the United States, then Black people, Black Jews, therefore, think it is outrageous to be talking about leaving the United States. Black Jews and non-Black Jews have become comfortable in sin and around sin. This is what happened in Egypt of old with God's people. Jacob/Israel and his children and their families should have left Egypt of old after the (7) seven year period of drought and famine, but they decided to stay in Egypt of old and be partakers of its sins.

They, the people of God, the children of Israel, copied the people in all of its ways. This was in direct disobedience to what God had told them not to do. They, the children of Israel, of Egypt of old, even started worshipping their god's. Like as God's people in the United States during these days. Satan has made it more acceptable/ easier to worship the idol gods, since the United States has labeled itself as the so-called Christian Nation, by disguising the idolatry; by presenting the idolatry under other names; such as, patriotism, loyalty, allegiance, psychiatrist, inspiration, being a fan, spirituality, mental health, etc. God's people during these days in the United States, worship the god's:

1. Christmas and Santa Claus, the Sun god
2. Easter, the Spring goddess
3. the Stature of Liberty and Flag of the United States
4. the golden stature of the Oscar
5. the dark world of Halloween
6. Movie Star
7. Certain Singers
8. the Pope of the Catholic Church
9. the Television
10. the Computer
11. the Cell Phone
12. the Pastor of a Church
13. the Gun
14. Sport, Certain Athletes

15. the Politician
16. the President
17. the Car
18. Money
19. Satan
20. Psychiatrist, Witch, Wizard/Warlock, Psychic
21. Etc.

You might say, I do not believe that the people of the United States worship all these things and people. The worshippers of much of the idolatry listed above, are called fans. We say this. Anything or any person that you put before God Almighty, then you worship them. You have made it or that person your god.

Exodus Ch. 20, V. 3
"Thou shalt have no other god before me."

Matthew Ch. 6, V. 24
"No man can serve two masters: for either he will hate the one, and love the other; or he will hold to the one, and despise the other. Ye cannot serve God and mammon."

Revelation Ch. 9, V. 20
"And the rest of the men which were not killed by these plagues yet repented not of the works of their hands, that they should not worship devils, and idols of gold, and of silver, and of brass, and of stone, and of wood . . ."

The worship above of the Scripture of Revelation, is for sure of this day and time; even if you thought that the gods of the other Scriptures above were not; if you thought it, you were wrong. So, just like the pagans of old, the United States has its many gods. The worshippers of much of the idolatry listed above of the United States, are called fans. Are there those in the United States who call themselves fans?

All of this idolatry of the long list above, God's people of the United States have been partakers of. Refer to our Book "March Was When JESUS Was Born And Not Christmas". So, it is totally ridiculous to expect that God's Black Jews and non-Black Jews to voluntarily leave the United States. Yet, we MUST be persuasive to reverse this mentality and we will; we have prophecy on our side. God knows how to do it and he will.

Ezekiel Ch. 39, V. 28
". . . I have gathered them into their own land, and have left none of them any more there."

Just as God sent Moses to Pharaoh, saying, Let My People Go. That seemed like an impossible mission for Moses. Yet, Pharaoh Let God's People Go. So will it be in the United States. God will perform Great Miracles in the United States, until his people, Black Jews and non-Black Jews, exit the United States in a Great Exodus.

You might ask, how much time do we have to leave the United States? The people of God, Black Jews and non-Black Jews should be out of the United States before the Great Tribulation starts. When the Great Tribulation starts, the United States will be the slaughter house to kill God's people. The only ones who will not be persecuted, will be God's people and others, who take the 666 Mark of the (Anti-Christ) Beast. All that take the 666 Mark will go to hell and burn in the lake of fire.

<u>Revelation Ch. 14, Vs. 9-11</u>
". . . If any man worship the beast and his image, and receive his mark in his forehead, or in his hand, . . . he shall be tormented with fire and brimstone . . . And the smoke of their torment ascendeth up for ever and ever: and they have no rest day nor night, who worship the beast and his image, and whosoever receiveth the mark of his name."

We have written in several of our Books when the Great Tribulation will begin. Refer to our Books:

1. "Proof That Your Leaders Have Deceived You And The End Times"
2. "How Long Will It Be Until The End"
3. "When The End Will Come"
4. "What God Is Now Telling Prophets About The End Times"

5. "Words From God, By God Appearing To Us Or Just Talking To Us, For The End Times"
6. "God Said Black People In The United States Are Jews"

In our Book "God Said Black People In The United States Are Jews", we revealed to you that President Barack Obama will be removed from his Presidency by the (Anti-Christ) Beast, Pope John Paul II, Carol Josef Wojtyla and Former President Bill Clinton, the other Beast, the False Prophet. After the two remove him from Office, they will kill him (15th) fifteen months later. Immediately after they kill President Barack Obama, the Sixth Trumpet will be sounded by the Sixth Angel. After the events associated with the Blowing of the Sixth Trumpet, the Great Tribulation will begin.

<u>Daniel Ch. 7, Vs. 6 & 12</u>
"After this I beheld, and lo another, like a leopard, which upon the back of it four wings of a fowl; the beast had also four heads; and dominion was given to it. As concerning the rest of the beast, they had their dominion taken away; yet their lives were prolonged for <u>a season and a time."</u>

<u>Revelation Ch. 9, Vs. 13,16-18</u>
"And the sixth angel sounded . . . And the number of the army of the horsemen were two hundred thousand thousand . . . And thus I saw the horses in the vision,

and them that sat on them, having breastplates of fire, and of jacinth, and brimstone . . . and out of their mouths issued fire and smoke and brimstone. By these three was the third part of men killed . . ."

God has also revealed to us that after the Temple in Jerusalem is rebuilt, the daily sacrifices will be offered for 1010 days and then the (Anti-Christ) Beast, Pope John Paul II, Carol Josef Wojtyla, will stop the daily sacrifice. Thirty days after that, the Great Tribulation will start. Refer, also, to our Book, "The Ten Horns Of The Books Of Daniel And Revelation".

So, the Great Tribulation is not far away. President Barack Obama can be removed from his Presidency within three years. Once the Sixth Trumpet is sounded it is very unlikely that there will be much travel. Before the Sixth Trumpet is blown, the Fifth Trumpet must be sounded. During the events associated with the blowing of the Fifth Trumpet, it is very, very, unlikely that much travel will be taking place. During this time there will be a Great Plague all over the earth that will incapacitate most of mankind. All will be afflicted with this excruciating painful plague, except those who speak in tongues as God give the utterance. Refer to our Book "Five Month Desire To Die, But Not Possible When Fifth Angel Blows Trumpet".

Revelation Ch. 8, V. 1

"And the fifth angel sounded . . . they should be tormented for five months . . . And in those days shall men seek death and shall not find it; and shall desire to die and death shall flee from them."

Revelation Ch. 8, V. 4

"And it was commanded them that they should not hurt the grass of the earth, neither any green thing, neither any tree; but only those men which have not the seal of God in their foreheads."

So, it appears for any traveling to be done, it should be done before or by the Blowing of the Fifth Trumpet; except God does something super natural; like translating us. This probably has limited the amount of time to Exodus the United States to between (2) two and (3) three years.

We know then based on the above paragraph, that part of the judgment of God for the enemies of God's people must take place soon. This is the judgment that we mentioned in Chapter 2 of this Book that will soon happen to white folks. This is the judgment that my wife, Prophetess Sylvia Franklin, said that God told her about; that something bad will soon start happening to white people. This is the judgment that I prophesied about in Chapter 2 of this Book. I prophesied that there will be judgment in:

1. tornadoes/hurricanes/other weather destruction
2. poverty
3. drought
4. fire
5. sickness and disease
6. death and mourning

This is what I prophesied would soon start happening to white folks. In fact, some small portion of it has already started.

As it was in Egypt of old, God will recompense you for the slavery and oppression of his people, I prophesied. These above things in this paragraph will soon happen. In fact, some small amount has already started happening, but you have not seen anything yet in comparison of what will happen.

This first part of the judgment of the United States is why the statement is made by the United States, Babylon The Great, in Revelation Chapter 18. Here we see the United States in denial after all that has happen to her.

Revelation Ch. 18, V. 7
". . . she hath said in her heart, I sit a queen, and am no widow, and shall see no sorrow."

God said [ok] then,

Revelation Ch. 18, V. 8

"Therefore shall her plagues come in one day, death and mourning, and famine; and she shall be utterly burnt with fire: for strong is the God who judgeth her."

This final judgment will happen immediately after the Great Tribulation. You might say, I do not think that the Scripture of Revelation Chapter 18, Verse7, proves that the United States will be in hard times. Well, just keep reading we will convince you.

So, for those of you who are God's people, Black Jews and non-Black Jews, who are so in love with the United States, what you love about it now, will not be in the soon to happen future. This final judgment is what I told you about in Chapter 1 of this Book; the dream and visions, God being by my side, that we looking down on of the future; the visions the size of a football field.

So we, God's people, must start planning now to get out of the United States. You might ask, how can this many people, around (200,000,000) two hundred million, have an Exodus from the United States? We have said, God has said, that only (148,000) one hundred forty eight thousand will be saved, be in the First Resurrection, the so-called rapture, in the United States; however, if you are in the United States and leave out of the United States, you could be saved; even around (200,000,000) two hundred million of Black Jews and non-Black Jews.

<u>If there was (148,000) one hundred forty eight thousand saved in the United States and you happened to be the other (1) one who was trying to be saved, you would not be if you were in the United States.</u> Therefore your chances of getting saved, being in the First Resurrection, the so-called rapture, is greatly enhanced by leaving the United States.

You might ask, where could around (200,000,000) two hundred million people go? You might ask, what other place could take on the influx of around (200,000,000) two hundred million people? Well, the obvious place is Africa. We, most of us of the around (200,000,000) two hundred million came from Africa and Africa we could return. Africa is where we should return.

This around (200,000,000) two hundred million Black Jews and non-Black Jews will not have to go into Africa as lacking refuges, but as a people of substantial means. This was the case when the children of Israel left Egypt of old. This, also, was the case when the children of Israel left the Great Babylon. Egypt of old was the super power of its day, like as the United States is the super power of the world now. Babylon The Great was the super power of its day, like as the United States is the super power of the world now. Refer to our Books:

1. "United States In The Bible"
2. "The Judgment Of The United States"

3.   "The Ten Horns Of The Books Of Daniel And Revelation"

Exodus Ch. 12, Vs. 30-32 & 35-36
"And Pharaoh . . . called for Moses and Aaron by night, and said . . . take your flocks and herds, as ye have said and be gone . . . And the children of Israel did according to the word of Moses, and they borrowed of the Egyptians jewels of silver, and jewels of gold, and raiment: And the LORD gave the people favour in the sight of the Egyptians, so that they lent unto them such things as they required. And they spoiled the Egyptians."

Ezra Ch. 1, Vs. 5-11
"Then rose up the chief of the fathers of Judah and Benjamin, and the priests, and the Levites, with all them whose spirit God had raised, to go up to build the house of the LORD which is in Jerusalem. And all they that were about them strengthened their hands with vessels of silver, with gold, with goods and with beasts, and with precious things, beside all that was willingly offered. Also Cyrus the king brought forth the vessels of the house of the LORD, which Nebuchadnezzar had brought out of Jerusalem, and had put them in the house of his gods; Even those did Cyrus king of Persia bring forth by the hand of Mithredath the treasurer, and numbered them unto Sheshbazzar the prince of Judah. And this is the number of them; thirty chargers of gold,

a thousand chargers of silver, nine and twenty knives, Thirty basons of gold, silver basons of a second sort four hundred and ten, and other vessels a thousand. All the vessels of gold and silver were five thousand and four hundreds. All these did Sheshbazzar bring up with them of the captivity that were brought up from Babylon unto Jerusalem."

Exodus Chapter 12, Verses 35 and 36, proves that the United States will fall on hard times.

Exodus Ch. 12, Vs. 35 & 36
"And the children of Israel . . . spoiled the Egyptians."

Not only that, there will soon be a Great Depression over the whole earth that will make the Great Depression of the (20's) twenties in the United States, seem like nothing. This Great Depression will happen because of the events associated with the Blowing of the First Five Trumpets. Refer to our Books:

1. "How Long Will It Be Until The End"
2. "When The End Will Come"
3. "Proof That Your Leaders Have Deceived You And The End Times"
4. What God Is Now Telling His Prophets About The End Time"
5. "Words From God, By God Appearing To Us Or Just Talking To Us, For The End Times"

6.   "Five Month Desire To Die, But Not Possible When Fifth Angel Blows Trumpet"

This Great Depression will happen during President Barack Obama's Presidency and before he is removed from Office by the (Anti-Christ) Beast, Pope John Paul II, Carol Josef Wojtyla and Former President Bill Clinton, the other Beast, False Prophet.

For those who are not among the around (200,000,000) two hundred million of Black Jews and non-Black Jews, if you help facilitate the Exodus, it will increase your chance of being among the (148,000) one hundred forty eight thousand that will be saved, in the First Resurrection, the so-called rapture, in the United States. This is true providing that you get born again. I know that there are some good white folks here in the United States. The white folks who have not been a party to the oppression of God's Black Jews, Black people, here in the United States. White people have actually help Black people in the United States; White folks who have been sympathetic to the struggle for justice toward Black People in the United States. These are those who God has chosen to help Black People in the United States. These are those who we mentioned in Chapter 1 and Chapter 2 of this Book. You white folks that I mentioned above have a good chance of being among the (148,000) one hundred forty eight thousand to be saved in the United States; providing that you get born again and obey God's word; your chances of being in the First Resurrection, the so-called rapture, would be greatly increased by helping God's Black Jews and non-Black Jews to leave the United States in the Great Exodus. Also, for those of you white folks who are not good, it is also benefit to you that you facilitate the Great Exodus of God's Black Jews and non-Black Jews from the United States. The sooner that we are gone from the United States, the sooner God's judgment against you can stop. Understand, many of those who have already got born again, will soon lose the Holy Ghost. So says God. Not only that, no one will be receiving the Holy Ghost/Spirit soon. God told my wife, Prophetess Sylvia Franklin, that who will be saved, he is saving now. Also, the Scriptures of Revelation Chapter 9, let us know that no one will get saved after a certain time.

Revelation Ch. 9, Vs. 13,18,20 & 21

"And the sixth angel sounded . . . the third part of men were killed . . . And the rest of the men which were not killed by these plagues yet repented not of the works of their hands, that they should not worship devils, and idols of gold, and silver, and brass, and stone, and of wood: which neither can see, nor hear, nor walk: Neither repented they of their murders, nor of their sorceries, nor of their fornication, nor of their thefts."

The above Scripture said that they "yet repented not"; if you do not repent you cannot get saved. As we told you earlier, that you MUST speak in tongues to get saved, to be in the First Resurrection, the so-called rapture. So, this points out another lie of those two lying ministers of Satan, that we mentioned in Chapter 1 of this Book. These two lying ministers say that you cannot speak in tongues until the people of God is called up before the (Anti-Christ) Beast during the Great Tribulation. What a lie! God himself revealed to me that you MUST speak in tongues to be saved, be born again, be born of God, to be in the First Resurrection, the so-called rapture.

I will now testify of what God told and showed me regarding speaking in tongues and being born again. When I first got saved, born again, as we have said, I spoke in tongues. I also was baptized in the name of JESUS. However, at this time I did not understand that by these two, was how you got born again, born of God. About a little over a year after I spoke in tongues, God told me to preach his word. I was an Electrical Engineer and this seemed so unlike me to do such a thing. This seemed so unlike what I would do. Well, after having being totally convinced that it was God who was telling me to preach, over a period of about six months, I began to preach. I had spoke in tongues and learned through God's word and had seen the evidence, that you have power when you speak in tongues; when you are born of the Spirit. This is what I thought that speaking in tongues meant; having all or some of the (9) nine gifts of the Spirit.

I Corinthians Ch. 12, Vs. 7-10

"But the manifestation of the Spirit is given to every man to profit withal. For to one is given by the Spirit the word of wisdom; to another the word of knowledge by the same Spirit; To another faith by the same Spirit; to another the gifts of healing by the same Spirit; To another the working of miracles; to another prophecy; to another discerning of spirits; to another divers kind of tongues; to another the interpretation of tongues . . ."

Well, I wanted those of my immediate family and relatives to know about this power related to speaking in tongues. All of my immediate family and relatives did not believe in speaking in tongues; they were Baptist. They believed that those who spoke in tongues had a devil doing it. All of my folks for generation after generation, were Baptist. In fact, my folks established the first church in the area where they live; a Baptist Church. My folks lived in a Community called Dawes in Mobile, Alabama of the United States.

I, at the time, when God told me to preach, lived in Montgomery, Alabama of the United States. During this time, I had recently got married to my wife, Prophetess Sylvia Franklin. Having this almost obsession to have people learn about the Holy Ghost/Spirit, I called my family and the Pastor of their Baptist Church for them to allow me to preach at their Church. I had already told my family and relatives that I spoke in tongues and they thought I had lost my mine. When I called them to let me preach at their Church, they agreed. I was shocked! It was like I was in a daze! The impossible was possible! The impossible was a reality! The only way I could explain this, is that they must have wanted to hear what this dreadful sinner had to say. For indeed I had been known as a terrible sinner among my immediate family, relatives and friends; even known as a terrible sinner to my acquaintances; even known as a terrible sinner to those who had heard of me.

Well, I set up an appointment for me to preach at that Baptist Church. Well, my wife and I went to Mobile and Dawes for me to preach. Nearly everyone who lived in Dawes was my immediate family, relatives, friends or close acquaintances.

Well, I was introduced in the Church as a preacher. I imagine that all wanted to sniggle, as they looked at each other. Well, I preached about speaking in tongues for about an hour. After preaching, I did what I had seen preachers do on television. I asked if anyone wanted to be saved; I said, I understand that most or nearly all in the Church are saved, but just in case there is one who is not saved, I ask you to repeat after me. So, I quoted Romans Chapter 10, Verse 9 and I declared to those who repeated after me and believe those words, that they are saved.

Romans Ch. 10, V. 9

"That if thou shalt confess with thy mouth the Lord Jesus, and shalt believe in thine heart that God hath raised him from the dead, thou shalt be saved."

Well, as my wife and I were driving back home to Montgomery, every time I thought about preaching, it was like a dagger was pushed into my heart and twisted. Every time I thought about the word of God, it was like a dagger was pushed into my heart and twisted. This repeated itself over and over and over again. Finally God said that I had lied to that Baptist Church on salvation. I was devastated! I was shocked! I had lied to my mother, sisters, brother, grandmother, aunts, uncles, first cousins, second cousins, other relatives, friends, and that Baptist Pastor. I was disappointed. I had let my God down. It was silence in that car to we got to Montgomery. When we pulled up into our driveway at our house, God said to me get your Bible. What God showed me, had not happened at one time, in such detail, before or since that time. As we entered into the house, God told me to open up my Bible. Well, I am not going to go into details. I am going to make it short. God led me through several Scriptures to show me the truth. Part of this counsel, was God told me to read John Chapter 3, Verse 8.

John Ch. 3, V. 8

"The wind bloweth where it listeth, and thou hearest the sound thereof, but canst not tell whence it cometh, and whither it goeth: so is every one that is born of the Spirit."

God said that the hearing in the above Scripture, is speaking in tongues. It says, "thou hearest the sound thereof . . . so is every one that is born of the Spirit".

God, also, during this time, showed me through the Scriptures, that the proper way to get baptized is to get baptize in the name of JESUS; unlike what 90% plus of the so-called Christians do; they baptize saying the titles of God rather his name; they baptize saying the titles Father, Son and Holy Ghost/Spirit. That is why their baptism do not remit sins. That is why they are so sinful; even having homosexuals among them. Refer to our Book" The Door Is Closing On The Last Opportunity For Immortality".

Let us get back to the around (200,000,000) two hundred million Black Jews and non-Black Jews leaving the United States. The other benefit of the around (200,000,000) two hundred million leaving the United States, is the possibility that if you do not be in the First Resurrection, the so-called rapture you have a chance of going into the millennium period as a mortal human being. The possibility is small however.

Isaiah Ch. 24, V. 6

"Therefore hath the curse devoured the earth, and they that dwell therein are desolate; therefore the inhabitants of the earth are burned, and few men left."

We, however, strongly urge you to be born again and obey God's word so you will be in the First Resurrection, the so-called rapture. Not only will you have to be among the "few men left", but also you must have to escape taking the 666 Mark of the (Anti-Christ) Beast, to go into the millennium.

Revelation Ch. 13, Vs. 15-16

". . . as many as would not worship the image of the beast should be killed. And he causeth all, both small and great, rich and poor, free and bond, to receive a mark in their right hand, or in their foreheads: And that no man might buy or sell, save he that had the mark, or the name of the beast, or the number of his name."

Revelation Ch. 20, Vs. 4 & 5

". . . and I the souls of them that were beheaded for the witness of Jesus, and for the word of God, and which had not worshipped the beast, neither had received his mark upon their foreheads, or in their hands . . ."

So, your chances of going into the millennium as a mortal human being is slim. So, just get born again and obey God's word; so you can be in the First Revelation, the so-called rapture.

You do not have to wait to leave the United States in the Great Exodus, to be born again and to obey God's word. In fact, we urge you not to wait. Why not wait, you might ask? You do not know when you are going to die. If you die before you get born again, you will go to hell and eventually to the lake of fire, where you will burn for ever and ever more.

Revelation Ch. 18, V. 4
"And I heard another voice from heaven, saying, Come out of her my people, that ye be not partakers of her sins, and ye receive not of her plagues."

Part of the sins that you would be partakers of, if you stayed in the United States and did not get born again and obey God's word, is that, you will be among those who would be persecuting God's people, his saints.

Of course, part of these sins would be that you would be a sodomite/homosexual and a witchcraft worker. In these last days, as we have written before in other of our Books, that the earth will be covered with two main spirits; the spirit of witchcraft and the spirit of sodomy/homosexuality. Refer to our Books:

1. "Words From God, By God Appearing To Us Or Just Talking To Us, For The End Times"
2. "The Whole World Becoming As Sodom"

All on earth during that time will be a witchcraft worker; who will not be in the First Resurrection, the so-called rapture. All on earth during that time will be a sodomite/homosexual; who will not be in the First Resurrection, the so-called rapture. So, if you are not a homosexual/sodomite and do not want to become one, you better get born again and obey God's word so that you can be in the First Resurrection, the so called rapture.

You might ask, what about the few that will go into the millennium? Will they be sodomites/homosexuals? The answer is no.

Isaiah Ch. 24 V. 6

". . . inhabitants of the earth are burned, and few men left."

There will be some few on earth during that time, who are so isolated, that they do not depend on the world's systems, and who did not take the 666 Mark; possibly, but they will not be homosexuals/sodomites. Maybe in Africa you might find some who are so isolated who will not take the 666 Mark and who are not homosexuals/sodomites; who are not born again.

However, God will yet use Cain's off spring, even during the Millennium. So, among the few that will be left on the earth after the wrath of God will be Cain's off spring. Although during the Battle of Armageddon only a six part of Russia will be left. We believe that this will be those of Russia who are in opposition to sodomites/homosexuals. We believe that this is why Vladermir Puttin, the Leader of Russia, Gog, the Leader of Magog, has instituted policies against homosexuals/sodomites. God made him do it.

Proverbs Ch. 21, V. 1
"The king's heart is in the hand of the LORD, as the rivers of water: he turneth it whithersoever he will."

Ezekiel Ch. 39, Vs. 1-4 & 6
"Therefore thou son of man, prophesy against Gog, and say, Thus saith the Lord GOD; Behold I am against thee, O Gog, the chief prince of Meshech and Tubal: And I will turn thee back, and leave but the sixth part of thee . . . And I will smite thy bow out of thy left hand and cause arrows to fall out of thy right hand. Thou shall fall upon the mountains of Israel . . . And I will send a fire on Magog, and among them that dwell careless in the isles: and they shall know that I am the LORD."

Revelation Ch. 20, Vs. 7-9

"And when the thousand years are expired, Satan shall be loosed out of his prison, And shall go out to deceive the nations which are in the four quarters of the earth, <u>Gog and Magog</u>, to gather them to battle: the number of whom is as the sand of sea. And they went on the breath of the earth, and compassed the camp of the saints about, and the beloved city: and fire came down from God out of heaven, and devoured them."

CAIN! CAIN! CAIN!

Even after God is so merciful to the off spring of Cain to allow them to go into the millennium and to live a thousand years; even after God himself teaches them for a thousand years; even after God for a thousand years allowed them not to be influenced by Satan; the off spring of Cain yet gravitate to their true choice of a god, Satan. Therefore, God Almighty/JESUS has mercy on them no more and destroy them all.

Revelation Ch. 20, Vs. 7-9

"And when the thousand years are expired, Satan shall be loosed out of his prison, And shall go out to deceive the nations which are in the four quarters of the earth, <u>Gog and Magog</u>, to gather them to battle: the number of whom is as the sand of the sea. And they went on the breath of the earth, and compassed the camp of the saints about, and the beloved city: and fire came down from God out of heaven, and devoured them."

For those like Martin Luther King who thought that the off spring of Cain, white folks, could or would change, the above proves otherwise. This is why God said that man that would be saved he chooses them. Otherwise, none of Cain's off spring would be saved.

John Ch. 15, V. 19
". . . I have chosen you out of the world . . ."

The above just reinforces what we said earlier in this Book in Chapter 1, that those that are good white folks, God chose you to be so. God chose you to do his will. God chose you to help his Black Jews.

Some might yet say, I do not believe that the United States will kill God's people. We are a God loving people, you might say. We say, the word of God says otherwise.

Revelation Ch. 18, Vs. 20 & 22
"Rejoice over her, thou heaven, and ye holy apostles and prophets; for God hath avenged you on her. And in her was found the blood of prophets, and of saints, and of all that was slain upon the earth."

Matthew Ch. 24, V. 10
"And then shall many be offended, and shall betray one another, and shall hate one another."

Revelation Ch. 18, V. 4
". . . Come out of her my people . . ."

You might ask, how are we going to get to Africa? How can around (200,000,000) two hundred million people get to Africa? You might ask, is God going to open up the Atlantic Ocean like he did the Red Sea for us to drive there? You might say, if God did that, then I would believe. If it would take all of that for you to believe, then consider yourself as being lost. You would not be among the (148,000) one hundred forty eight thousand or any other number that will be saved, be in the First Resurrection, the so-called rapture.

Revelation Ch. 18, V. 4
". . . Come out of her my people . . ."

There might be some that say, we will be glad for you Black people to leave the United States and go back to Africa. Well, those that say such, are very ignorant and naïve of how Capitalism works in the United States. Capitalism in the United States, for the most part, is a disguised form of slavery of Black people in the United States. This system of Capitalism would totally collapse without the Black people's over a trillion dollars per year of consumer spending. The real powers to be, "the big money" people, understand this. This is why the institutionalize effort to keep Black people struggling to survive has been established. This explains why Mitt Romney was going around, during the last Presidential Campaign, saying that President Barack Obama, who is half Black, did not have a clue of how the economy of the United States works. When you are struggling, you spend the money you have. Two thirds of the United States economy is based on consumer spending.

Rich people do not spend money on consumer spending. They already have what they need and want. Not only that, but there are very few of them.

So, unknowingly, we, Black people, Black Jews, are here in the United States against our will; we are captive. This captivity is rooted in mind control witchcraft. This mind control witchcraft is enhanced very greatly by the television media. The scenario is this. Have the captives to work to barely survive and let them have a television. While they are not working they can watch television. The television tells them that they are free; that they live in the best place in the world; that they should be grateful to live in the United States; that the United States is number one in every good thing; that people in the United States are just having good times all the time; that we make money by just playing games or having a good time; etc.

So, you go to work, watch television, about once a week, go spend the little money you have to get things you see on television, go to sleep and get back up to go the work. This is repeated over and over and over again; every day, every week, every month and every year. This is even repeated generation after generation. Let My People Go.

Revelation Ch. 18 V. 4
". . . Come out of her my people . . ."

This continual struggle by the Black people, Black Jews, also, ensure that there is a continual work force for the "big money" people. As we mentioned in Chapter 2 of this Book, those that are rich benefit from having those who struggle.

Let My People Go! Let My People Go!

Revelation Ch. 18, V. 4
". . . Come out of her my people . . ."

God speaks right now, COME OUT OF HER MY PEOPLE, THAT YOU BE NOT CONSUMED! I SEND YOU MY WORD, says God!

Amos Ch. 3, V. 7
"Surely the LORD God will do nothing, but he revealeth his secret unto his servants the prophets."

<u>Isaiah Ch. 42, V. 9</u>

"Behold the former things are come to pass, and new things do I declare: before they spring forth I tell you of them."

My wife, Prophetess Sylvia Franklin, several years ago had a dream. It was a short dream. In the dream, God showed her that Former President Bill Clinton sent for me. She believe it was in Washington, D. C. or New York City where I was to meet him. So I went to meet the Former President Bill Clinton. We had a relative short conversation. After that she, my wife, said that Former President Bill Clinton was cold acting toward me; he shunned me.

About six or seven years ago, God showed both my wife, Prophetess Sylvia Franklin and my son, Daniel Isaiah Franklin, that Former President Bill Clinton would be over the United States again. God, also, told me this same thing before that time. Refer to our Book "New York City Becomes The Capitol Of The New World Order".

Could this visit with Bill Clinton be as when Pharaoh did with Moses, before the children of Israel left Egypt of old in the Exodus. Pharaoh's attitude toward Moses was somewhat of a shun also. He told Moses to go away from him.

Exodus Ch. 12, Vs. 31 & 32
"And he called for Moses and Aaron by night, and said, Rise up, and get you forth from amongst my people, both you and the children of Israel; and go, serve the LORD as ye have said. Also, take your flocks and your herds, as ye have said, and be gone."

Let us say something about God opening up the Atlantic Ocean as He did with the Red Sea. Some have said that God did not even open up the Red Sea. They have said that it is nothing except Bible fiction of this event. They have said that the Movie, "The Ten Commandments", portrayal of the Red Sea being open, is nothing more than fantasy. The portrayal by the "The Ten Commandments" Movie is a good portrayal of what actually happened of God opening up the Red Sea. You haters of the Almighty God, but worshippers of idol gods, we tell you, we choose to believe the Almighty God's word.

Exodus Ch. 14, Vs. 15,16,21 & 22
"And the LORD said unto Moses . . . lift thou up thy rod, and stretch out thine hand over the sea, and divide it . . . And Moses stretched out his hand over the sea; and the LORD caused the sea to go back by a strong east wind all that night and made the sea dry land, and the waters were divided. And the children of Israel went into the midst of the sea on dry ground: and the

waters were a wall unto them on their right hand, and on their left."

We not only have God's word on this, but God, also, let us know that such a thing took place, by a dream he gave unto me. In the dream, about (11) eleven years ago; there were ministers in Mobile, Alabama laying out on mattresses in the Mobile Bay; they were around the area in the Bay near the causeway; these were the ministers who had or once had the Holy Ghost; then I got my mattress too and laid out on it, also, in the Mobile Bay; but when I laid down on my mattress I began to sink, water then covered me; so, I got my mattress and moved to another spot in the Bay and when I laid down on my mattress, I began to sink and water covered me; so, I got my mattress and moved between two of the ministers that were laying down on their mattresses; as I laid down on my mattress, I again began to sink and water covered me; then God spoke to me and said that I could not be like the rest of the sleeping ministers; then God took me out of the Mobile Bay and then God caused the water of the Bay to be rolled back into a very high wall; it kind of looked like the scene in "The Ten Commandments" Movie, when the water rolled back for the children of Israel to go through the Red Sea; then God spoke to me and said that all I had to do is speak and people will receive the Holy Ghost; he said the Holy Ghost would be given like a rushing flood, just as when the wall of water would be released; God said, however, someone would get hurt, just as when the wall of water when released would hurt those ministers that were laying out sleeping on their mattresses in the Bay.

It has not happened yet, that we know of, that when I speak many multitudes of people will be filled with the Holy Ghost. Maybe this will be one of the Great Miracles that God will perform for the Great Exodus to take place from the United States.

Revelation Ch. 18, V. 4

". . . Come out of her my people . . ."

Due to the publication of this Book, God will cause all of our Books to be spread throughout the earth; thereby causing his word to be spread throughout the earth. This will help fulfill the word from God given to me on May 31, 2002 at 9:00 p.m. God told me that I will establish his Church in these last days; I think, only his Smyrna Church and not the Church of Philadelphia.

Revelation Ch. 2, Vs. 8-10

"And unto the angel of the church in Smyrna write; These things saith the first and the last, which was dead and is alive; I know thy works, and tribulation, and poverty, (but thou art rich) and I know the blasphemy of those who say they are Jews, and are not, but are of the synagogue of Satan. Fear none of those things which thou shall suffer: behold, the devil shall cast some of you into prison, that ye may be tried; and ye shall have tribulation ten days: be thou faithful unto death, and I will give you a crown of life."

The reason God said that we would be in poverty in the above Scripture, is because we will not take the 666 Mark of the (Anti-Christ) Beast.

Revelation Ch. 13, Vs. 17-18
"And that no man might buy or sell, save he that had the mark, or the name of the beast, or the number of his name. Here is wisdom. Let him that hath understanding count the number of the beast: for it is the number of a man; and his number is Six hundred threescore and six."

We tell you how the name of the beast is equal to 666 in our Book "The Name Of The (Anti-Christ) Beast And 666 Identification". Yes, we tell you how God told us how Pope John Paul II, Carol Josef Wojtyla, is equal to 666.

The Church of Philadelphia is the 144,000 Jews, only virgins, of the Book of Revelation. The Book of Revelation says they are of "little strength" because there are only 144,000 of them. God himself told me this in June of the Year 2002 when we were having a revival at our Church.

Revelation Ch. 3, Vs. 7-10

"And to the angel of the church in Philadelphia write; These things saith he that is holy, he that is true, he that hath the key of David, he that openeth, and no man shutteth; and shutteth, and no man openeth; I know thy works: behold, I have set before thee an open door, and no man can shut it: for thou hast a little strength, and hast kept my word, and hast not denied my name. Behold, I will make them of the synagogue of Satan, which say they are Jews, and are not, but do lie; behold, I will make them to come and worship before thy feet, and to know that I have loved thee. Because thy hast kept the word of the patience, I also will keep thee from the hour of temptation, which shall come upon all the world, to try them that dwell upon the earth."

Revelation Ch. 14, Vs. 1,4-5

"And I looked, and lo, a lamb stood on the mount Sion, and with him an hundred forty and four thousand, having his Father's name written in their foreheads. These are they which were not defiled with women; for they are virgins. These are they which follow the Lamb whithersoever he goeth. These were redeemed from among men, being the firstfruits unto God and the Lamb. And in their mouth was found no guile: for they are without fault before me and the throne of God."

The Church of Philadelphia will not be persecuted during the Great Tribulation. The Church of Smyrna will be persecuted during the Great Tribulation.

<u>Revelation Ch. 12, Vs. 13-17</u>
"And when the dragon saw that he was cast out unto the earth, he persecuted the woman which brought forth the man child. And to the woman was given to wings of a great eagle that she might fly into the wilderness, into her place, where she is nourished for a time, and times, and half a time, from the face of the serpent. And the serpent cast out of his mouth water as a flood after the woman, that he might cause her to be carried away of the flood. And the earth helped the woman, and the earth opened her mouth, and swallowed up the flood which the dragon cast out of his mouth. And the dragon was wroth with the woman, and went to make war with the remnant of her seed, which keep the commandments of God, and have the testimony of Jesus Christ."

The Smyrna Church and the Philadelphia Church of the Book of Revelation, are the only ones of the Seven Churches that will be saved; be in the First Resurrection, the so-called rapture. Refer to our Books:

1. "Words From God, By God Appearing To Us Or Just Talking To Us, For The End times"
2. "Understanding The Book Of Revelation To Understand The Book Of Revelation"

3.   "Events Of The Seven Seals And The Coinciding End Time Events Mentioned Elsewhere In The Bible"

4.   "What God Is Now Telling His Prophets About The End Times"

The fact that the saints of God, God's holy people, the people who get born again and obey God's word, will in the very soon future not have any money, means that we should be planning for that time right now. God will use the Great Depression that we mentioned earlier in this Book for his saints benefit. God will bless his saints before that time with large sums of money. We should use this money to purchase things during the Great Depression. We can buy things during that time very cheaply that will help us out during the Great Tribulation; when we will not be able to buy or sell. This will fulfill the Scripture written by King Solomon.

Proverbs Ch. 13, V. 22
". . . and the wealth of the sinner is laid up for the just."

So, when God's people, Black Jews and non-Black Jews, exit the United States in the Great Exodus, with the spoils from the United States, we should use this riches to buy things during the Great Depression. This is one of the main reasons why God will cause the Great Depression.

Exodus Ch. 12, V. 36
". . . And they spoiled the Egyptians."

Remember this, the Great Depression will happen during President Barack Obama's time in Office. It will happen before he is removed from Office by the (Anti-Christ) Beast, Pope John Paul, Carol Josef Wojtyla and the other of the two Former President Bill Clinton, the other Beast, False Prophet. It, the Great Depression, will happen in around two years from now.

Revelation Ch. 18, V. 4
". . . Come out of her my people . . ."

We believe that one of the Great Miracles that God will perform to convince the Black Jews and non-Black Jews to leave the United States, is that God will heal all of us of whatever that might be wrong with us. This is what God did when he brought the children of Israel out of Egypt of old.

Psalm 105, Vs. 36-38
"He smote also all the firstborn in their land, the chief of all their strength. He brought them forth also with silver and gold and their was not one feeble person among their tribes. Egypt was glad when they departed: for the fear of them that fell upon them."

It seems even yet that it will take more than has been said to convince God's Black Jews and non-Black Jews to leave the United States. Even though we have said that God healed all of his people coming out of the Egypt of old. You might say, it is nothing wrong with me, so God healing all of his people leaving the United States is not an attractive lure for me. Not only that you might say, my mother is in good health; my father is in good health; my sister(s) is/are in good health; my brother(s) is/are in good health; my nieces and nephews are all in good health. Not only that you might say, we are very well situated financially. So we love it in the United States, you might say.

Well, God surely knew all of this when he said that all of his people, Black Jews and non-Black Jews, will leave the United States in a Great Exodus. Not only will the non-Jews want you to leave the United States, but God has designed even another convincer in the situation to get his people out of the United States. Well, we believe that the event associated with the Sounding/Blowing of the Fifth Trumpet will be this convincer. Remember, this will be a time on all the earth when all, except those who speak in tongues, will be tormented with an excruciating painful plague for a five month period.

Revelation Ch. 9, Vs. 1-6

"And the fifth angel sounded, and I saw a star fall from heaven unto the earth: and to him was given the key to the bottomless pit. And he open the bottomless pit; and there arose a smoke out of the pit, as the smoke of a great furnace; and the sun and air were darkened by reason of the smoke of the pit. And there came out of the smoke locusts upon the earth: and unto them was given power, as the scorpions of the earth have power. And it was commanded them that they should not hurt the grass of the earth, neither any green thing, neither any tree; but only those men which have not the seal of God in their foreheads. And to them it was given power that they should not kill them, but that they should be tormented five months: and their torment was as the torment of a scorpion, when he striketh a man. And in those days shall men seek death, and shall not find it; and shall desire to die and death shall flee from them."

We believe that during this time is when God will heal them all; heal all of the Black Jews and non-Black Jews leaving the United States. For God to heal them of the excruciating painful plague, you will be glad to leave the United States. For this excruciating painful plague to end, by God's people, who are Jews, leaving the United States, then the non-Jews would be glad for the Jews to leave the United States. When we say "believe" we only say it because we have not receive, yet, multiples of confirmation from God. We require for our writings when we say something having only one word from God without confirmation, we say we believe. We know that we are wring the future and it must be true what we say!

Psalm 105, V. 38
"Egypt was glad when they departed: for fear of them that fell upon them."

After all that will fall upon the United States due to judgment of God, this excruciating painful plague will be the last convincer to cause his people to leave the United States. You might say, I thought that the Scriptures of Revelation Chapter 9, said and you said, that everyone would have this excruciating painful plague except you speak in tongues. We believe that this will be the fulfillment of the dream that I had that we mentioned earlier in this Chapter, when I was in the Mobile Bay. God said at that time, that all I had to do is speak and multitudes will be filled with the Holy Ghost. It seems very plausible that this might be this time; after all this was a time when the water was rolled back as during the Great Exoodus of God's people from Egypt of old.

Romans Ch. 11, V. 24
"For if thou wert cut out of the olive tree which is wild by nature, and wert graffed contray to nature into a good olive tree: how much more shall these, which be natural branches, be graffed into their own olive tree."

The Scripture said that the only ones that will not suffer this excruciating painful plague would be those who have the seal of God. If you are filled with the Holy Ghost, you speak in tongues. You cannot have the seal of God except you speak in tongues. Refer to our Book "Five Months Desire To Die, But Not Possible When Fifth Angel Blows Trumpet". Also, refer to the Scriptures in the Book of Ephesians.

Ephesians Ch. 4, V. 30
"And grieve not the holy Spirit of God, whereby ye are sealed unto the day of redemption."

You might say, I thought you had to be born of water as well as the Spirit to be saved, be in the First Revelation, the so-called rapture. You are right. We believe that there is enough water in the Atlanic Ocean and rivers of Africa to accomplish Baptism of a Great multitude.

Daniel Ch. 12, V. 10
"Many shall be purified, and made white, and tried; but the wicked shall do wickedly: and none of the wicked shall understand; but the wise shall understand."

Being "purified, and made white," in the above Scripture, means to be baptized.

We use to could never understand why God cause this excruciating painful plague. We believe God told us why on September 7, 2013, while writing this Book. As I walked into our bathroom, I believe that God told me the purpose of the Blowing of Fifth Trumpet. In fact, I believe that God told me this a few days earlier. The excruciating painful plague is to get the Black Jews and non-Black Jews out of the United States.

Remember, we told you that the Sounding/Blowing of the Fifth Trumpet will be during President Barack Obama's Presidency before he is removed from Office. As said earlier in this Book, he will be removed from Office by Pope John Paul II, Carol Josef Wojtyla and Former President Bill Clinton, the other Beast, the False Prophet. This will be around (2) two years from now.

We have said that there will be very, very, little travel during this time of the Sounding of the Fifth Trumpet. This means that God will have to do something super natural to get Black Jews and non-Black Jews out of the United States; maybe even opening up the Atlantic Ocean. Remember what we said about when we use the word "believe". The (5) five month period of this plague, we believe, will be the time it takes to complete the Great Exodus.

COME OUT OF HER MY PEOPLE! COME OUT OF HER MY PEOPLE! NOT ONLY BEING MY PEOPLE

APOSTLE FREDERICK E. FRANKLIN'S TESTIMONY

Let me give you my personal testimony. Let me tell you about how I got filled with the Holy Ghost. Back in 1985 I lived in Washington, D.C. I was not married at that time. It was in October of 1985. I had my own business as a Utilities Engineering Consultant. As a sinner and as usually was the case, I left out of a certain bar around 1:00 am. When finally I reached the place where I was living and was opening my door, the telephone began to ring. I went in and answered the telephone. It was my first cousin calling from Mobile, Alabama. He, also, was about high and was just getting in from a bar. As usually was the case, we started talking about God. We knew little to nothing about God, but somehow we always started talking about God. As we talked, I started talking about the preachers of God. I said that those O lying preachers that say they lay hands on people and they get healed are the worst ones. I said only Jesus could heal someone like that. I at least knew that Jesus could heal like that. My cousin said you are right. Two drunks talking. He then said the only other ones who could do that were Peter, John, Paul and the other Apostles of the Holy Bible. I was shocked. I was so shocked that I got sober. I said what! What! He said yes! Peter, John, Paul and the other Apostles laid hands on the people and they got healed. I was totally astounded! I was totally amazed! I was sober!

After we hanged up the telephone, I went and picked up the Bible which I had kept with me since about 1963. I had never opened the Bible I was just religious and kept it with me. I had been putting off reading it for all these years. When the urge would come to me to read it, I would put it off to the next month, or next week, or next day, or when I finished a certain project, or when I finished during this or that. I did not know it then, but I know now, the urge was God trying to get me to read the Bible. I finally dusted off and opened that Bible. It was now around 2:00 am. I wanted to see for myself where it said that a man could lay hands on a person and he or she could get healed. I was after all, an Electrical Engineer and this was illogical. How could flesh, blood and bones heal someone? It did not make any sense. Not having any idea where to look, I searched and searched and searched. I read and read and read. Finally, somewhere between 3:00-4:00 am, I found it. I saw that Peter laid hands on people and they got healed. It was amazing! It was like a very bright light was turned on in my head. I was speechless. To understand the greatness of my astonishment, you need to understand my childhood hopelessness. I, as a child, being black brought up in Alabama, living far out in a rural area, started working when I was four years old. I would go outside of our house at night, walking through the woods, looking up in the sky at the moon and the stars, and ask God why? I knew it had to be a God. I would ask God why would he leave his children down on this earth at the mercy of Satan? Satan of course, I knew, had no mercy. I could not understand why. Everything that seemed to be good, appeared to be on Satan's side. The evil people had it. White folks had it who were doing evil. Why, why, why, was my question? I never received an answer. It appeared that God could care less about the suffering of and in justice to his children on this earth.

When I saw that someone could get healed by another just by laying hands on them, then I understood clearly the answer to my why. I understood that God had not left us at the mercy of Satan. I, however, wanted to see could anyone lay hands on people and they could get healed. As I continued to search and read, now about day break, I "discovered" that you had to have the Holy Ghost to be able to heal. I wanted then to see could anyone receive the Holy Ghost. Now far in the morning of the next day, I "discovered" that anyone could receive the Holy Ghost. I "discovered" that you spoke in tongues when you received the Holy Ghost. My life desire would never be the same again. I wanted to see how I could receive the Holy Ghost. I learned that you had to repent. So, I asked God to forgive my sins. Then I ask God to give me the Holy Ghost, let me speak in tongues. Nothing happened. I did not speak in tongues. All that day I was asking God to forgive my sins and to let me speak in tongues. I did not work that day. This went on all day and into the night. Nothing ever happened. Exhausted I fell asleep into the next morning. When I woke the next day I started doing the same thing. I asked God to forgive my sins and let me speak in tongues. Nothing happened. I thought that maybe I need to read God's word and then I might receive the Holy Ghost. So, I read several Books of the Bible. Then I asked God to forgive my sins and let me speak in tongues. Nothing happened. I did this over and over each day and nothing ever happened. I had stop working all together. To receive the Holy Ghost was the most important thing in my life. I made a pledge to God that I would not go to the bars again. Nothing happened as I sought for the Holy Ghost. I made a pledge to God to stop drinking and stop smoking marijuana. Nothing happened. I made a pledge to God to stop fornicating. Nothing happened as I sought for the Holy Ghost. I was praying for the Holy Ghost and reading God's word and nothing happened. I decided to read the whole Bible. I read from Genesis through the Book of Revelation and nothing happened as I sought for the Holy Ghost during that time. Now it was the end of the year of 1985 and nothing happened as I sought for the Holy Ghost. I decided to move from Washington, D.C., back to my house in Montgomery, Alabama. Now after reading the whole Bible, I was praying about (22) twenty two hours a day to receive the Holy Ghost and nothing happened. I

APOSTLE Frederick E. Franklin

started crying and praying and nothing happened. I had only cried (4) four times in my life. I remember all the way back from (2) two years old. Crying and seeking for the Holy Ghost is all I did. I never spoke in tongues. This crying and seeking God for the Holy Ghost reached now into August of the year 1986. I had counted all of the months, weeks, and days to that time of seeking for the Holy Ghost, now seeking about (22) twenty two hours a day. I had about (3) three months before, cleaned out my house of everything that I thought was sinful. I threw away all pornography, whiskey, wine and beer, marijuana and whatever I thought was sinful into my trash can. I did this and nothing ever happened. Now here it was in August, seeking to speak in tongues and I had not. I said, I thought, that maybe I need to join a Church. This might would help, I thought. I looked into the yellow pages of the phone book and chose (4) four churches that I would check out to join. This was now August 3, 1986. I was still seeking God for the Holy Ghost. I still was crying and praying to speak in tongues about (22) twenty two hours a day. On August 3, 1986, I turned on my television early in the morning and turning the channels I saw and heard some ridiculous sounding Church Choir singing with the TV camera shaking. I stopped to see what in the world would this be on television so unprofessional. I was amazed. I had once worked at a television station in Cleveland, Ohio, and I was just amazed at this. As I looked and listened in amazement, a young woman came before

She told me to go and tell the Apostle. I went to the Apostle and said I want to receive the Holy Ghost. He said Oh, I thought you already had the Holy Ghost. He said come back, either next Sunday or that afternoon before the 6:00 taping of the radio broadcast, and he would pray for me to receive the Holy Ghost. I said that I would come back before the taping of the broadcast. I was not about to wait for a whole week. I could tell you how many months, weeks and days I had been seeking for the Holy Ghost. I had been seeking for the Holy Ghost every day since October of 1985 and it was now August 10, 1986.

When I went home from Apostle Tumlin's Church, The All Nations Church of God, I did something that was key to me receiving the Holy Ghost. Remember I told you that I threw away all, pornography, whiskey, wine, beer, marijuana and other things I thought was sinful into my trash can. Well, I went back to my trash can and I got (2) two marijuana joints out of it and brought them back into my house. I had stop smoking marijuana during my time of seeking the Holy Ghost and had no intentions of smoking anymore. I did not know it at that time, but I know it now, it was Satan that convinced me to get those (2) two joints out of my trash can. I thought, Satan told me, that I might need them if I got a headache. I just had them in my closet in case I might need them for a headache. The Devil, Satan, just made a fool out of me. The only time I had those headaches is when

I had a hangover. I was not going to have a hangover because I had stop drinking. What a fool. However, on August, 10, 1986, before I went back to receive the Holy Ghost, it had to be God who told me, I went to my closet and got those two joints and flushed them down my toilet stool. When I did this, it felt like a very, very, heavy weight was taken off me. At 5:00 on August 10, 1986, I was back at Apostle Tumlin's Church, The All Nations Church of God, to receive the Holy Ghost. I went in the Church and sat down in about the fourth row of the pews, next to the aisle, on the left side looking from the pulpit. There were about (3) three to (4) four people in the sanctuary, including the Apostle's wife. They were there praying. However, the Apostle was nowhere to be seen. I sat there waiting for the Apostle and he never showed up. It was now 5:30 pm and there was no sign of the Apostle. I was getting very anxious because the radio broadcast's taping was to start at 6:00 pm. Finally, the Apostle came out of a room from the front of the Church. I was so excited! I finally was going to receive the Holy Ghost! The Apostle walked towards me and down the aisle and right by me and went into the rest room near the entrance to the Church. He did not say one word to me. Not even a gesture toward me. Some minutes past by and he was still back there. I just kept praying. I just kept repenting. Finally he came out. He came to the back of me and put his hands on my head and said receive the Holy Ghost. I was excited and nervous. I did not know what to expect. Then with his hands on my head, he said speak in tongues. I said to myself, what is this man talking about? I said to myself, you have to receive the Holy Ghost before you speak in tongues. He, the Apostle, just kept saying speak in tongues. Then he, with hands on my head, started speaking in tongues. Then he said receive the Holy Ghost, speak in tongues. Then he started speaking in tongues. Then he said speak in tongues with his hands on my head. Then to my amazement he began to give up on me and remove his hands, I stood up so his hands could not be removed. I thought to myself, no, no, you are not going to give up on me this quick. So he let his hands stay on my head and began to speak in tongues. Then he said speak in tongues. I by this time, with the Apostle's hands on my head, was standing in front of the church facing the pews, but I did not know it. He said again speak in tongues. I said to myself this is not working, I am going to get out of here. I said to myself, the next time that he speaks in tongues I am just going to mimic him and pretend that I have the Holy Ghost so I can leave. He then spoke in tongues. Then I went to mimic him. The next thing I knew, I was speaking in a language that sounded like Hebrew, before the audience of people in the Church, motioning my hands like I was before them teaching them something. Then I said to myself, what in the world am I doing. This was totally unlike me. Then the Apostle said, you have been filled with the Holy Ghost. Then all of a sudden I stop speaking this Hebrew like language. The Apostle just kept saying you have been filled with the Holy Ghost. I was saying to myself, is this what it is to be filled with the Holy Ghost? I did not know what to say. I did not know what to think. I went and sat back down in the same place that I was sitting before. By this time, it was time for the taping of the radio broadcast. As I sat there, Satan began to talk to me. He told me that I did not have the Holy Ghost. He said that as evil as I had been, that God would not give me the Holy Ghost. Satan then brought up to me every evil thing that I had done. He kept saying, you do not have the Holy Ghost. This went on for about an hour as I sat there. After the taping was over and I left the Church, Satan kept up his accusations and saying that I did not have the Holy Ghost. All the way as I drove home, he kept it up. When I entered into my house I said to God that if I received the Holy Ghost, let me know without a shadow of doubt. Immediately I began to speak in tongues. I was speaking loud in tongues. I began to analyze this speaking. I was not trying to mimic. My mouth and tongue were moving and I was not trying to make them move. I was speaking sounding eloquently, whatever I was speaking. This speaking went on for about an hour with me analyzing to see whether it was me or God speaking. I then thought that I might not be able to stop speaking in tongues. Immediately I stop speaking in tongues and God spoke to me clearly and said that my name had been written in the Book of Life and everything has been worth it. I knew what God meant by worth it and I started crying. All of these months. All of these weeks. All of these days. All of the praying. All of the crying. All of this seeking for the Holy Ghost, but it is worth it. Later on I would get baptized by the Apostle in the name of Jesus Christ for the remission of my sins.

This one thing I want to point out. I could have received the Holy Ghost, all the way back in October of 1985, if I had got rid of that dope and the other things of sin. You cannot hold on to the past, anything of the past that is sin, and receive the Holy Ghost. Satan would have caused me to go to hell over (2) two marijuana joints. Two joints would have kept me from immortality.

PROPHETESS SYLVIA FRANKLIN'S TESTIMONIES OF RECEIVING THE HOLY GHOST

When my wife, Prophetess Sylvia Franklin, was a child she had a very depressing life. There was constant arguing and fighting between her father and mother. Her father would be drunk and pull out a gun and threaten to kill her mother and even at certain times to kill her and her brother.

At (10) ten years old, Sylvia would look out of her window and look up and ask God to take away the gloom and let the sun shine. She always would do this. It always seemed to be so gloomy in those days. As time went by in this constant state of family turmoil, at (13) thirteen years old, God did let the sun shine in Sylvia's life. After Sylvia, her mother and brother started attending a small Holiness Church, Sylvia was involved with a street meeting service. This was Apostle William Tumlin's Church. During the meeting the people were singing and praising the Lord. Sylvia then started singing and praising the Lord and all of a sudden she started speaking in tongues.

Not really understanding what had happened to her, Sylvia was in and out of Church. As time passed Sylvia lost the Holy Ghost. At (17) seventeen years old Sylvia was in a service at Apostle William A. Tumlin's Church, All Nations Church of God. While singing and praising was taking place in the Church, Apostle Tumlin came to where Sylvia was and laid hands on her head and she started speaking in tongues. She was restored in the Holy Ghost. Later on she got baptized by Apostle Tumlin in the name of Jesus Christ for the remission of sins. Sylvia's life was never the same again.

OUR OLDEST CHILD ELIJAH JEREMIAH EZEKIEL FRANKLIN'S TESTIMONY OF RECEIVING THE HOLY GHOST

On January 31, 1995 our son, Elijah Jeremiah Ezekiel Franklin, had his fifth birthday. This is the same child the doctors said would have only a ten percent or less chance of being born. This is the same child some would have recommended being aborted (murdered in the womb). This is the same child who is in very good health. This is the same child the doctors said would have probable extreme health problems. This is the same child who was born premature.

After turning five years old, two days later on February 2, 1995, while we (Frederick and Sylvia) were praying for him in our house during our weekly Thursday night prayer service, he was filled with the Holy Ghost. He spoke in tongues for about an hour. After he finished speaking in tongues, we baptized him in the name of Jesus.

Through the testimony of Elijah's salvation, other children have desired to be saved and were indeed filled with the Holy Ghost and baptized in the name of Jesus.

<u>NOTE THIS</u>. Two Days After Elijah Spoke In Tongues, He Prophesied And Said, God Is Saying To Him, That We Would Be Moving To A Farm In Mobile, With Farm Animals. Later On That Year, In October, We Moved To That Farm.

DANIEL ISAIAH FRANKLIN'S AND REBEKAH ANNA FRANKLIN'S TESTIMONIES OF RECEIVING THE HOLY GHOST

This dedication is to give praise and glory to God Almighty, Father Jesus our Lord and Savior and to his Son Jesus Christ of whom the Father dwelled in on this earth, for the born again experience of Daniel Isaiah and Rebekah Anna.

June 15, 1998 was a special day in our family. This is the day that we completed household salvation in our family, the day that we could say that all five of us were born again. On this day, June 15, 1998, as we all prayed fervently during our daily dedicated afternoon prayer, God moved mightily in our presence. We were already excited for the young woman that we had prayed to receive the Holy Ghost the past night which we were preparing to baptize after our prayer time.

As we prayed fervently for God to move in a special way that day for the souls to be saved in our community, God spoke to us to pray for Daniel and Rebekah. We, Frederick, Sylvia and Elijah, started praying for them to be filled with the Holy Ghost. As we prayed, we noticed that Daniel and Rebekah were under the influence of the presence of God in praising him and they began to speak in tongues. We wondered could this actually be happening this fast as we had been praying for? Could our five year old son and four year old daughter now finally be filled with the Holy Ghost? We had been praying to God every day since they were conceived in Sylvia's womb for them to receive the Holy Ghost. We didn't really know whether they were speaking in tongues or not at this time because during prayer our children often would mimic us when we were speaking in tongues. But, this time seemed to be different, especially with Rebekah. Daniel Isaiah, every since he was about one year old, always has fervently praised the Lord, singing, dancing, lifting up his hands to God and appearing to speak in tongues. Rebekah, however, did not normally praise God as enthusiastically as did Daniel. But on this day, June 15, 1998, at about 2:00 p.m., our little Rebekah was on fire! And even the normally enthusiastic Daniel seemed to have a double portion. We looked at them and wondered could this actually be it? Could our Daniel Isaiah be filled with the Holy Ghost? Could our son, who was born three months premature, be now born again of the Spirit? Could our son, who at one time only weighed (2) two pounds and (13) thirteen ounces, be born again of the Spirit? Could our son, who the doctors said would have to stay in the hospital for at least three months after he was born, who only stayed one month because he was so healthy, could he actually be speaking in tongues?

231

rightly so, for not knowing our son was already filled with the Holy Ghost, our joy was rekindled and we went immediately and baptized Daniel Isaiah and Rebekah Anna in the name of Jesus for the remission of their sins to complete their born again experience.

REASONS TO WANT
TO BE SAVED

Why would you want to be saved? Well, I will give you three good reasons to want to be saved. You might say, I don't need to be saved. You might say, I'm doing just fine like I am. Well, you might have an argument if you could guarantee the future would be what you want it to be. You might have an argument if you could guarantee that you will be living next year. You might have an argument if you could guarantee that you will be living next month. You might have an argument if you could guarantee that you will be living next week. You might have an argument if you could guarantee that you will be living tomorrow. You might have an argument if you could guarantee you will not die today. You might have an argument if you could guarantee that you will not die the next hour. You might have an argument if you can ensure that you will be living the next five minutes. If you had control over your time of life, you might not need Jesus' salvation. But, since Jesus, the God Almighty, has control over your appointed time of life, if you are not totally stupid, then you should realize that you need to be saved.

This is the bottom line, either ignorance or stupidity causes you not to get saved. Jesus, the God Almighty, before the world was created, assigned an appointed time for each of us to be born. He, also, set the exact time of our death. Jesus has assigned us our parking meter of life. Who is familiar with a prepaid cell phone? Well, for a prepaid cell phone, you have an allotted amount of minutes to use your cell phone. Once you have used all of your minutes, it is useless. It is dead. Well, Jesus, the God Almighty, has assigned us our prepaid cell phone of life. Do you know how many minutes you have left? Supposed you have (15) fifteen minutes left. Suppose (10) ten. Suppose (5) five. Do you know whether an earthquake will now occur at this place or not? Do you know whether an airplane will now or not crash into this building? Do you know whether a terrorist will now or not blow up this building? Jesus knows. Do you know whether you will or will not fall dead in this minute of a heart attack? Do you know on the way from here whether you will have an head on collision with another vehicle and be killed? Jesus knows. Your time clock of life is running out!

The number one trick of Satan is to convince those that are not saved, who want to be saved, that you have more time, until your parking meter of life expires. He hopes to convince you that you have more time, until your prepaid cell phone of life is used up.

You might be one of the fools that might say, that you do not care whether you die without being saved. If this is you, you are indeed a fool. One of the main reasons to get saved is to stay out of hell. If you are one of the ones that say you do not care whether you die without being saved, then you probably do not understand that there is a hell with a wide opened mouth waiting to swallow you. Hell is a real place. When death occurs, you, the real you, your soul, will either go to hell or heaven. If you are saved, you go to heaven. If you are not saved, you go to hell. What is hell, you might ask? Hell is a place where souls are tormented with fire. A very, very, very, hot fire. The hottest fire that we can make on earth, spirits can touch it, walk in, lay on, etc., without it burning them. Spirits are beings that include angels and devils. God, also, is a spirit. Hell is so hot that it burns spirits. Not God, but other Spirits. A person's soul is spirit. A person's soul is the person's desire, feeling, emotions, mind, hearing, sight, taste, smell and memory. The real person. The real you. The body dies and rots. The soul is eternal. It will live either in hell or with God, forever and ever more. Hell is a place located in the center of the earth. Those that are in hell are in continual torment. They are burning continually. There is no relief. Just continual screaming and burning. No rest day nor night. There is no water. There is no air conditioner. There is no fan. There is no kind of cooling. Remember, understand, that they have their feelings in hell. Remember, understand, that they have their desires in hell. Their desire to quench their thirst can never be satisfied. Their desire to alter their circumstances can never be done. Their desire to leave hell will never be fulfilled. They will be in their forever. Their cry out to God for help will be in vain. Hopelessness! Hopelessness! Hopelessness! Pain of burning continually. The pain from a burning fire, if not the worst, is one of the worse pains that you can have. Pains on your hands. Pains on your feet. Pains on your arms. Pains on your legs. Pains on your back. Pains on your belly. Pains on your chest. Pains on your face. Pains on your ears. Pains on your tongue. Pains on the top of your head. Pain everywhere. Pains all the time. All day and all night forever and ever and ever and ever and evermore. They had an alternative, they had another choice, they could have gotten saved.

This is the second good reason to want to get saved. For those of you that believe that there is a God, then you should want to be saved for your love to God. You know that God is a good God, the good God. You know that God has been good to you. You cannot live without God. You cannot walk without God. You cannot talk without God. You cannot eat without God. You cannot sleep without God. You cannot love without God. You cannot be loved without God. You cannot breathe without God. All of these things and many, many, other good things God provides you. And, not only you, but all others even his enemies. Even those that curse him. Even those who prefer to serve Satan rather than God himself. It was God who protected you from death. It was Satan who tried to kill you. It was God who healed you. It was Satan that made you sick. It was Satan who killed your love ones. It was God who protected your love ones from Satan that allowed them to live as long as they did.

To get saved is to show your love and gratitude to God. To get saved is to show your love and gratitude to God for a price that he paid for your salvation. The price was very great. God allowed his Son Jesus of Nazareth to die. There have been some men who have allowed their sons to die for what they considered a good cause or for a friend. God allowed his son to die for his enemies. God, even, allowed his Son to suffer for his enemies. To suffer such suffering never suffered before. Unbearable sufferings. God allowed him to be slapped. God allowed him to be spit on. God allowed his beard to be pulled off of his face, causing pain and bleeding and swelling. God allowed a crown made of thorns to be put on his head. Shoved into his scalp and forehead, causing pain, bleeding and swelling. God allowed his Son to be beat with (39) thirty-nine strokes of a whip that would snatch the meat off his bones. Pain, excruciating pain, bleeding and swelling. God allowed him to be nailed on a tree in his hands and feet, causing pain, excruciating pain, bleeding and swelling. God saw his son suffer. He saw his body bleed, from the top of his head to the bottom of his feet. God saw his Son's body swell, from the top of his head to the bottom of his feet. God saw his Son's body from the top of his head to the bottom of his feet change to a painful black and blue-like color with pain and red with blood. He saw him agonize in pain and misery, until through the bleeding and swelling he was not recognizable as a man. We would not and could not allow our sons and daughters, who we loved, to suffer even for a friend, let along their enemies. All that God has done for us, so much, and He only requires for a token of love, for us to accept his glorious salvation. For us to stay out of hell. So, for those who believe that there is a God, God Almighty, then our love for God should make us want to be saved. To get saved is to show that God's sacrifice of His Son was not in vain with us. This salvation of ours makes God's investment yield a return. So great investment for such a little return. Without your salvation the little return is even smaller. Just think, by getting saved, the God that created the universe will allow us to be with him for ever and ever more. It will not be just any existence, but God has promised us in the Holy Bible, that we will have no more sorrow, no more pain, no more crying and no more death. I believe that God has allowed me to experience how it will be in heaven. Not long after I was filled with the Holy Ghost, while living in Montgomery, Alabama, God gave me a visitation. While sitting in my bed, with my legs and my feet in the bed, eyes wide opened, the presence, the glory, the anointing of God, moved on me. I felt it. I knew somehow it was God. I don't know how I knew, but I knew without a shadow of doubt that it was God. The sensation, the feeling, started at the bottom life benefit, consider this. Soon in these days, there will be a great tormenting plague to cover the whole earth. This will happen very soon. Possibly, during George W. Bush's time as President. This torment will be excruciating pain. This pain will be continual. It will affect all ages, babies, young children, teenagers, young adults, middle age adults, senior citizens, all. The pain of this plague will be so horrible, until the people will want to die. People will want to commit suicide. There will be no medicine for cure. There will be no medicine for relief. There will be screaming all over the earth. The children will be screaming. The parents will be screaming. The grandparents will be screaming. The great grandparents will be screaming. The nurses will be screaming. The doctors will be screaming. Those of the police force will be screaming. Those of the army will be screaming. Those of the Air Force will be screaming. Those of the Navy will be screaming. Those of the Marines will be screaming. The members of the House of Representatives will be screaming. The Senators will be screaming. The Supreme Court Justices will be screaming. The Vice President will be screaming. The President will be screaming. The Pope will scream. All will scream!

All of this paining. All of this misery. All of this hurting and no relief. No relief for five months. Yes! It will last for (5) five months. And think about this. It is hard to get sleep when you are in pain. What hopelessness.

The curse of this plague will be so bad that people will want to die. However, the curse of this plague will not allow them to die. This curse has been told about in the Book of Revelation of the Holy Bible. Turn to the Book of Revelation in your Bible. Look at Chapter (9) Nine. Read Verse (6) Six.

Revelation Ch.9, V.6
"And in those days shall men seek death, and shall not find it; and shall desire to die and death shall flee from them."

This great excruciating painful plague will soon happen. This painful plague will be the closest thing to hell itself. It will be so horrible, so excruciating, that God told me to write a book about it to warn the people. This is the book here. The name is "Five Month Desire To Die, But Not Possible When Fifth Angel Blows Trumpet." The only ones on planet Earth that will not be affected with this great painful plague, will be those that have the Holy Ghost. You must have the Holy Ghost to be saved. All that have the Holy Ghost speak in tongues.

If you, yet, after reading this, due to some custom, tradition or religion, do not get saved, it is because you are too stupid to get saved.

THE FOUR EASY STEPS TO GET SAVED/BORN AGAIN:

1. Repent:

   a. ask God to forgive your sins, ask in the name of Jesus;
   b. surrender your will for God's will to be done in your life.

2. Ask God to save you, to fill you with the Holy Ghost, ask in the name of Jesus.

2. Do not ask God anymore to save you, just thank God, praise God for saving you. You must thank God in the name of Jesus. At the point of your greatest sincerity, you will speak in another language. This will be your sign of confirmation. God will be using your mouth to speak a language spoken somewhere on earth that you have not learned. This is your sign that you are born of the Spirit.

3. Get baptized in the name of Jesus Christ.

John Ch.3,Vs.3&5

"Jesus answered ... Except a man be born again, he cannot see the kingdom of God . . . Jesus answered . . . Except a man be born of water and of the Spirit he cannot enter into the kingdom of God."

John Ch.3,V.8

". . . thou hearest the sound thereof . . . so is everyone that is born of the Spirit."

Colossians Ch.3,V.17

"And whatsoever ye do in word or deed, do all in the name of the Lord Jesus . . ."

LIST OF BOOKS THAT
WE HAVE WRITTEN

1. Proof That **YOUR LEADERS** Have **DECEIVED YOU** And The End Times
2. What **GOD** Is Now Telling His Prophets **ABOUT** The **END TIMES**
3. Five Month **DESIRE TO DIE**, But Not Possible When Fifth Angel Blows Trumpet
4. **GOD's** Word Concern **MARRIAGE AND DIVORCE**
5. The Name Of The (Anti-Christ) Beast And **666** Identification
6. **WHERE GOD's PEOPLE** (Saints) **GO** When GOD Comes Back To Get Us
7. How You Can **PROVE** That **YOU HAVE** A **SOUL**
8. **JESUS** Was **NOT CRUCIFIED WHEN** As Has Been **TAUGHT**
9. Reasons For **JEWS** To Believe That **JESUS** Is The **MESSIAH**
10. **THE** Big **LIE**
11. Proof: The **TRINITY** Doctrine **IS A LIE**
12. **UNITED STATES IN** The **BIBLE**
13. **HOW LONG** Will It Be **TO** The **END**?
14. **OBSTACLES TO** Saints Being **SAVED**
15. How Will **SAINTS** Make It **DURING** The **GREAT TRIBULATION**?

30. How Any Candidate Can **GET** The **VOTE FROM** GOD'S **PEOPLE**, Denominations And Catholics
31. The **LOST REVELATION**
32. **NEW YORK CITY** Becomes The **CAPITAL** Of The **NEW WORLD ORDER**
33. A Man Named **BUSH PREPARES** The **WAY FOR** The **ANTI-CHRIST**
34. **MARCH** Was When **JESUS** Was **BORN** And **NOT CHRISTMAS**
35. **GOD'S FOUR** Healings And Deliverances Which He **DESIRES FOR US**
36. The Parallel/Comparison Of **JEWS AND BLACK PEOPLE** Of The United States
37. The **CHRONOLOGICAL ACCOUNT** Of The Gospels Of What Is Said **ABOUT JESUS**
38. **TIMES** That **GOD APPEARED UNTO US**
39. The **WHOLE WORLD** Becoming **AS SODOM**
40. The **TWO** Main **REASONS CMMUNION** Is To Be **TAKEN**
41. The **DOOR IS CLOSING ON** The Last Opportunity For **IMMORTALITY**
42. **(CONFIDENTIAL—(ONLY FOR THE 15 APOSTLE) — "APOSTLES HANDBOOK** Of Ministry Tasks Before & During The Great Tribulation")
43. **WORDS FROM GOD** By God Appearing To Us Or Just Talking To Us, **FOR THE END TIMES**
44. **GOD SAID BLACK PEOPLE** In The United States **ARE JEWS**.

HOW TO GET SAVED

To Be Saved You must Speak with Tongues & Be Baptized in the Name of Jesus

John Ch. 3, V. 3

"Jesus answered . . . Except a man be born again, he cannot see the Kingdom of God."

John Ch. 3, V. 5

"Jesus answered . . . Except a man be born of water and of the Spirit, he cannot enter into the Kingdom of God."

Acts Ch. 2, V. 38

". . . Repent, and be baptized every one of you in the name of Jesus Christ for the remission of sins, and ye shall receive the gift of the Holy Ghost."

How to Repent: (1) Sincerely ask God to forgive your sins, ask in the name of Jesus; (2) Surrender your will for God's Will to be done in your life.

After Repenting: Sincerely ask God to save you, to give you his Spirit, to give you the Holy Ghost, to have you to speak with other tongues. [Once you have asked, then just continue to thank God for doing so, just praise him, sincerely. You WILL then speak in tongues.]

<u>John Ch. 3, V. 8</u>
". . . thou hearest the sound thereof . . . so is everyone that is born of the Spirit."

<u>After Speaking in Tongues</u>: Get baptized in the name of Jesus, again you must be repented.

<u>NOTE</u>: You can be baptized and then receive the Holy Ghost or be filled with the Holy Ghost then be baptized.

<u>Speaking in Tongues</u>: Speaking in tongues (unknown language) is God speaking through you.

<u>Mark Ch. 16, V. 17</u>
"And these signs shall follow them that believe . . . they shall speak with new tongues."

<u>Acts Ch. 2, V. 4</u>
". . . and began to speak with other tongues as the Spirit gave them utterance."

<u>Acts Ch. 22, V 16</u>
". . . be baptized, and wash away thy sins . . ."

<u>Colossians Ch. 3, V. 17</u>
"And whatsoever ye do in word or deed, do all in the name of the Lord Jesus . . ."

The name of the Father is Jesus, the name of the Son is Jesus, the name of the Holy Ghost is Jesus.

John Ch. 17, V. 26
"And I have declared thy name unto them . . ."

John Ch. 5, V. 43
"I am come in my Father's name . . ."

Hebrews Ch. 1, V. 4
". . . he hath by inheritance obtained a more excellent name . . ."

John Ch. 4, V. 24
"God is a Spirit . . ."

Question: Is the Father Holy? Answer: Yes. God is a Father; God was manifested in flesh as a Son; God is a Spirit, the Holy Spirit, the Holy Ghost.

I, Frederick E. Franklin, am a Father, am a Son, am a Human Being. Father, Son, Holy Ghost and Father, Son, Human Being are titles. God's name is Jesus.

Matthew Ch. 28, V. 19
". . . Teach all nations, baptizing them in the name of . . . the Son . . ."

TO BE A PART OF THE F&SF MINISTRY FOR JESUS THE FOLLOWING WILL BE EXPECTED

II Timothy Ch.2, V.3

"Thou therefore endure hardness, as a good soldier of Jesus Christ."

Ephesians Ch.6, V.10

". . . be strong in the Lord, and in the power of his might."

Ephesians Ch.5, V.27

"That he might present it to himself a glorious church, not having spot, or wrinkle, or any such thing; but that it should be holy and without blemish."

The F&SF Ministry For JESUS Soldier Will:

1. Be Filled With The Holy Ghost (Evidenced By Speaking In Tongues)
2. Be Baptized In The Name Of JESUS
3. Be Honest And Sincere
4. Have Love And Compassion For Others
5. Properly Pay Tithes And Give Offerings
6. Believe In One God (The God Of Abraham, Isaac, And Jacob)

7. Worship Only God Almighty, The Creator Of The Universe, JESUS
8. Be Holy
9. Attend Sabbath (Friday Dark To Saturday Dark) Service(s)
10. Attend Other Service(s) When Possible
11. Make Continuous Sincere Efforts For Souls To Be Saved
12. Profess/Testify That You Must Speak In Tongues And Be Baptized In The Name Of Jesus To Be Saved
13. Profess/Testify That The Great Tribulation Is Before The Rapture
14. Reveal That Pope John Paul II Is The (Anti-Christ) Beast
15. Be Bold (Not A Coward)
16. Desire To Grow In Revelation And Power Of God
17. Be Faithful And Dedicated To The F&SF Ministry For JESUS
18. Receive/Accept The Teachings Of Apostle Frederick E. Franklin
19. Not Espouse Teachings/Doctrines Contrary To That Of Apostle Frederick E. Franklin
20. Adhere To The Leadership Of Apostle Frederick E. Franklin
21. Not Be A Liar
22. Not Be A Hypocrite
23. Not Be A Witchcraft Worker
24. Not Be A Partaker Of Idolatry

EXCERPTS FROM OUR BOOK "THE NAME OF THE (ANTI-CHRIST) BEAST AND 666 IDENTIFICATION"

There will be great deception. The scriptures indicate that the (Anti-Christ) Beast, Pope John Paul II, Carol Josef Wojtyla, will fake his death. Later on, to fake being resurrected from the dead. All to the end, to fake that he is God. All to the end, to discredit JESUS' resurrection. All to the end, to discredit that JESUS is God and rather to show/deceive that he is God.

<u>Revelation Ch. 17, V. 8</u>
". . . the beast that was, and is not, and yet is."

The Above scripture indicates that the Beast, Pope John Paul II, Carol Josef Wojtyla, was living. It further indicates that he will seem not to be living, but he actually will be living. He was living. He appears not to be living. But, he yet is living.

JESUS IS GOD

1. <u>I John Chapter 5, Verse 20</u>
"And we know that the Son of God is come, and hath given us an understanding, that we may know him that is true, and we are in him that is true, even in his Son Jesus Christ. This is the true God, and eternal life."

2. <u>John Chapter 1, Verses 1 & 14</u>
"In the beginning was the Word, and the Word was with God, and the Word was God. And the Word was made flesh, and dwelt among us, (and we beheld his glory, the glory as of the only begotten of the Father,) full of grace and truth."

3. <u>I Timothy Chapter 3, Verse 16</u>
"And without controversy great is the mystery of godliness: God was manifest in the flesh, justified in the Spirit, seen of angels, preached unto the Gentiles, believed on in the world, received up into glory."

4. <u>Isaiah Chapter 9, Verse 6</u>
"For unto us a child is born, unto us a son is given: and the government shall be upon his shoulder: and his name shall be called Wonderful, Counsellor, The mighty God, The everlasting Father, The Prince of Peace."

5. Matthew Chapter 1, Verse 23

"Behold, a virgin shall be with child, and shall bring forth a son, and they shall call his name Emmanuel, which being interpreted is, God with us."

6. Titus Chapter 1, Verses 3 & 4

". . . God our Saviour; . . . the Lord Jesus Christ our Saviour."

7. Isaiah Chapter 43, Verse 11

"I, even I, am the Lord; and beside me there is no Saviour."

8. Isaiah Chapter 44, Verse 6

"Thus saith the Lord the King of Israel, and his redeemer the Lord of hosts; I am the first, and I am the last; and beside me there is no God."

9. Revelation Chapter 1, Verses 17 & 18

". . . I am the first and the last: I am he that liveth, and was dead . . ."

10. Revelation Chapter 22, Verses 13 & 16

"I am Alpha and Omega, the beginning and the end, the first and the last. I Jesus have sent mine angel to testify unto you these things in the churches . . ."

11. Isaiah Chapter 44, Verse 24

"Thus saith the Lord, thy redeemer, and he that formed thee from the womb, I am the Lord that maketh all things; that stretcheth forth the heavens alone; that spreadeth abroad the earth by myself . . ."

12. <u>Colossians Chapter 1, Verses 16, 17 & 18</u>
"For by him were all things created, that are in heaven, and that are in earth, visible and invisible, whether they be thrones, or powers: all things were created by him, and for him: And he is before all things, and by him all things consist. And he is the head of the body the church."

13. <u>Ephesians Chapter 5, Verse 23</u>
"For the husband is the head of the wife, even as Christ is the head of the church: and he is the saviour of the body."

14. <u>Colossians Chapter 2, Verse 9</u>
"For in Him dwelleth all the fullness of the Godhead bodily."

15. <u>I John Chapter 5, Verse 7</u>
". . . three that bear record in heaven, the Father, the Word, and the Holy Ghost: and these three are one."

16. <u>Revelation Chapter 15, Verse 3</u>
". . . Great and Marvelous are thy works, Lord God Almighty; just and true are thy ways, thou King of saints."

17. <u>Revelation Chapter 17, Verse 14</u>
". . . and the Lamb shall overcome them: for he is Lord of lords, and King of kings; and they that are with him are called, and chosen, and faithful."

18. <u>I Thessalonians Chapter 3, Verse 13</u>
". . . God, even our Father, at the coming of our Lord Jesus Christ with all his saints."

19. <u>Zechariah Chapter 14, Verse 5</u>
". . . and the Lord my God shall come, and all the saints with thee."

20. <u>I John Chapter 3, Verse 16</u>
"Hereby perceive we the love of God, because he laid down his life for us."

21. Etc.

<u>THE FOUR EASY STEPS TO GET SAVED/BORN AGAIN</u>:

1.   Repent:

    a.   ask God to forgive your sins, ask in the name of Jesus;
    b.   surrender your will for God's will to be done in your life.

2.   Ask God to save you, to fill you with the Holy Ghost, ask in the name of Jesus.

3.   Do not ask God anymore to save you, just thank God, praise God for saving you. You must thank God in the name of Jesus. At the point of your greatest sincerity, you will speak in another language. This will be your sign of confirmation. God will be using your mouth to speak a language spoken somewhere on earth that you have not learned. This is your sign that you are born of the Spirit.

4.   Get baptized in the name of Jesus Christ.

John Ch.3,Vs.3&5

"Jesus answered . . . Except a man be born again, he cannot see the kingdom of God . . . Jesus answered . . . Except a man be born of water and of the Spirit he cannot enter into the kingdom of God."

John Ch.3,V.8

". . . thou hearest the sound thereof . . . so is everyone that is born of the Spirit."

Colossians Ch.3,V.17

"And whatsoever ye do in word or deed, do all in the name of the Lord Jesus . . ."

THE SABBATH

What Is The Sabbath?

The Sabbath is a holy day ordained by God to be so. It is a day for all to cease from work.

When Is The Sabbath?

The Sabbath is the last day, the seventh day of the week.

Genesis Ch.2, Vs. 1-3
"Thus the heavens and earth were finished, and all of the host of them. And on the seventh day God ended his work which he had made; and he rested on the seventh day from all his work which he had made."

Exodus Ch.20, Vs. 8-11
"Remember the sabbath day, to keep it holy. Six days shalt thou labour, and do all thy work: But the seventh day is the sabbath of the Lord thy God: in it thou shalt not do any work, thou, nor thy son, nor thy daughter, thy manservant, nor thy cattle, nor thy stranger that is within thy gates: For in six days the Lord made heaven and earth, the sea, and all that in them is, and rested the seventh day: wherefore the Lord blessed the sabbath day, and hallowed it."

<u>Exodus Ch.23, V. 12</u>

"Six days thou shalt do thy work, and on the seventh day thou shalt rest: that thine ox and thine ass may rest, and the son of thy handmaid, and the stranger, may be refreshed."

When Does The Day Start?

The day starts at dark and goes to the next day at dark.

<u>Genesis Ch.1, Vs 5, 8, 13, 19, 23 & 31</u>

". . . And the evening and the morning were the first day . . . And the evening and the morning were the second day. And the evening and the morning were the third day. And the evening and the morning were the fourth day. And the evening and the morning were the fifth day. And God saw every thing that he had made and, behold, it was very good. And the evening and the morning were the sixth day."

Is It A Sin To NOT Keep Or Violate The Sabbath?

To keep the Sabbath is one of the ten commandments. One of the ten commandments say thou shalt not kill. Another says thou shalt not steal. Just as it is sin to kill and steal, likewise, is it a sin to NOT keep or to violate the Sabbath.

Exodus Ch.20, V. 13-15
"Thou shalt not kill. Thou shalt not commit adultery. Thou shalt not steal."

What You Should Not Do On The Sabbath.

Exodus Ch.20, V. 10
"But the seventh day is the sabbath of the Lord thy God: in it thou shalt not do any work, thou, nor thy son, nor thy daughter, thy manservant, nor thy maidservant, nor thy cattle, nor thy stranger that is within thy gates . . ."

Nehemiah Ch.10, V. 31
"And if the people of the land bring ware or any victuals on the sabbath day to sell, that we would not buy it of them on the sabbath, or on the holy day . . ."

Nehemiah Ch.13, Vs. 16-18
"There dwelt men of Tyre also therein, which brought fish, and all manner of ware, and sold on the sabbath unto the children of Judah, and in Jerusalem. Then I contended with nobles of Judah, and said unto them, What evil thing is this that ye do, and profane the sabbath day? Did not your fathers thus, and did not our God bring all this wrath upon this city? Yet ye bring more wrath upon Israel by profaning the sabbath."

What Happened When The Sabbath Was Not Kept Or Violated Intentionally.

Numbers Ch.15, Vs. 32-36

"And while the children of Israel were in the wilderness, they found a man that gathered sticks upon the sabbath day. And they that found him gathering sticks brought him unto Moses and Aaron and unto all the congregation. And they put him in ward, because it was not declared what should be done unto him. And the Lord said unto Moses, The man shall be surely put to death: all the congregation shall stone him with stones without the camp. And all the congregation brought him without the camp, and stone with stones and he died; as the Lord commanded Moses."

Numbers Ch.15, Vs. 30-31

"But the soul that doeth ought presumptuously, whether he be born in the land, or a stranger, the same reproacheth the Lord; and that soul shall be cut off from among his people. Because he hath despised the word of the Lord, and hath broken his commandment, that soul shall be utterly cut off; his iniquity shall be upon."

Not Keeping Or Violating The Sabbath Out Of Ignorance.

Numbers Ch.15, Vs. 27-28
"And if any soul sin through ignorance . . . the priest shall make atonement for the soul that sinneth ignorantly, when he sinneth by ignorance before the Lord, to make atonement for him; and it shall be forgiven him."

Numbers Ch.15, Vs. 22, 24-25
"And if ye erred, and not observed at all these commandments . . . Then if it shall be, if ought be committed by ignorance without the knowledge . . . the priest shall make an atonement for all the congregation of the children of Israel, and it shall be forgiven them . . ."

Other Benefits Of Keeping The Sabbath.

God is pleased with those who obey his word and the promises of the Holy Bible is available to you.

Isaiah Ch.56 Vs. 2, 5-7
"Blessed is the man that doeth this, and the son of man that layeth hold on it; that keepeth the sabbath from polluting it, and keep his hand from doing any evil. Even unto them will I give in mine house and within my walls a place and a name better than the sons and daughters. I will give them an everlasting name, that shall not be cut off. Also the sons of the stranger that

join themselves to the Lord, to serve him, and to love the name of the Lord, to be his servants, every one that keepeth the sabbath from polluting it, and taketh hold of my covenant; Even them will I bring unto my holy mountain, and make them joyful in my house of prayer . . . their sacrifices shall be accepted upon mine altar; for mine house shall be called an house of prayer for all people."

Exodus Ch.23, V. 12
". . . thou shalt rest . . . be refreshed."

Exodus Ch.20, V.12
". . . the Lord blessed the sabbath day, and hallowed it."

Why Has Sunday Been Chosen As The So-Called Sabbath By The So-Called Christians And Some Christians?

The Pope of 325 A.D. birth this blasphemy of changing the Sabbath day from the seventh day to the first day of the week. This blasphemous change of the sabbath to Sunday was done to have the people worship God the Almighty on the same day as the worship of the sun god. Sunday the worship of the Sun god. This blasphemous change was prophesied of in the scriptures.

Matthew Ch.24, V. 24
"For there shall arise false Christs, and false prophets, and shall shew great signs and wonders; insomuch that, if it were possible, they shall deceive the very elect."

Daniel Ch.7, V. 25
"And he shall speak great words against the most High, and shall wear out the saints of the most High, and think to change times and laws . . ."

Daniel Ch.8, V. 12
"An host was given him against the daily sacrifice by reason of transgression, and it cast down the truth to the ground; and it practiced and prospered."

To justify this blasphemous change, he, the Pope, had to use scriptures of the Holy Bible. He used three places in the scriptures.

Matthew Ch.28, Vs. 1-6
"In the end of the sabbath, as it began to dawn toward the first day of the week, came Mary Magdalene and the other Mary to see the sepulchre. And, behold, there was a great earthquake: for the angel of Lord descended from heaven, and came and rolled back the stone from the door, and sat upon it. His countenance was like lightning, and his raiment white as snow; And for fear of him the keepers did shake, and became as dead men. And the angel answered and said unto the women,

Fear ye not: for I know that ye seek Jesus, which was crucified. He is not here: for he is risen, as he said. Come, see the place where the Lord lay."

Supposedly, because Jesus was resurrected on the first day of the week, the sabbath should be changed to the first day of the week.

I Corinthians Ch.16, Vs. 1-3

"Now concerning the collection for the saints, as I have given order to the churches of Galatia, even so do ye. Upon the first day of the week let every one of you lay by him in store, as God hath prospered him, that there be no gatherings when I come. And when I come, whosoever ye shall approve by your letters, them will I send to bring your liberality to Jerusalem."

Supposedly, because Paul told them to take up a collection on the first day of the week, this, therefore, means that the New Testament Church's sabbath is on the first day of the week.

Acts Ch.20, V. 7

"And upon the first day of the week, when the disciples came together to break bread, Paul preached to them, ready to depart on the morrow, and continued his speech until midnight."

Supposedly, because the disciples came together on the first day means that they came to hear the word, and because Paul preached on the first day, supposedly, this shows that the New Testament Church had as its sabbath the first day of the week.

What ridiculous justification(s) to change the Sabbath to the first day of the week.

Scriptures Of The New Testament Refuting The So-Called Sunday Sabbath.

Let us first look at the Pope's last so-called justification, Acts Ch.20, V. 7. When the scriptures said that they came "together to break bread," it means that they came together to eat. While they were there together, Paul took this opportunity to preached to them. Like any preacher would do. Refer to the immediate following scriptures, Acts Ch.20, Vs. 8-12.

Acts Ch.20, Vs. 8-12
"And there were many lights in the upper chamber, where they were gathered together. And there sat in the window a certain young man named Eutychus, being fallen into a deep sleep: and as Paul was long preaching, he sunk down with sleep, and fell down from the third loft, and was taken up dead. And Paul went down, and fell on him, and embracing him said, Trouble not yourselves; for his life is in him. When he therefore

was come up again, and had broken bread, and eaten, and talked a long while, even till break of day, so he departed. And they brought the young man alive, and were not a little comforted."

Let us now look at the Pope's I Corinthians Ch.16, Vs. 1-3, justification. Here Paul tells the Church of Corinth to give an offering to the Church in Jerusalem. He said take up collection on the first day of the week. Note that Paul said that there should not be any gathering. The people could not gather on the sabbath day to sell or give their goods or livestock to get a collection, so Paul said do it on the first day of the week. And whatever they gathered on the first day of the week, that is where their offering would come from.

Let us now look at the Pope's third and remaining justification, Matthew Ch.28, Vs. 1-6. These scriptures speak of Jesus' resurrection on the first day of they week. Somehow, this gives us the right to change God's word of a seventh day Sabbath. This is nonsense. God says that there is nothing above his word, not even the name of Jesus.

Psalm 138, V. 2
"I will worship toward thy holy temple, and praise thy name for thy lovingkindness and for thy truth: for thou hast magnified thy word above all thy name."

Now let us see when Paul, Jews and the Gentiles, the New Testament Church, really worshipped. When their Sabbath actually was.

<u>Acts Ch.18, V. 4</u>
"And he reasoned in the synagogue every Sabbath, and persuaded the Jews and the Greeks"

<u>Acts Ch.13, Vs. 13-17, 22-23, 42-44</u>
"Now when Paul and his company loosed from Paphos . . . they came to Antioch . . . and went into the synagogue on the sabbath day, and sat down. And after the reading of the law and the prophets the rulers of the synagogue sent unto them, saying, Ye men and brethren, if ye have any word of exhortation for the people, say on. Then Paul stood up, and beckoning with his hand said, Men of Israel, and ye that fear God, give audience. The God of this people of Israel chose our fathers . . . he raised up unto them David to be their King . . . Of this man's seed hath God according to his promise raised unto Israel a Savior, Jesus . . . And when the Jews were gone out of the synagogue, the Gentiles besought that these words might be preached to them the next sabbath. Now when the congregation was broken up, many of the Jews and religious proselytes followed Paul . . . And the next sabbath day came almost the whole city together to hear the word of God."

Note: Jews that worshipped God, only worshipped on the seventh day, the real Sabbath day.

I Peter Ch.3, Vs. 15-16

"But sanctify the Lord God in your hearts: and be ready always to give an answer to every man that asketh you a reason of the hope that is in you with meekness and fear: Having a good conscience; that, whereas they speak evil of you, as of evildoers, they may be ashamed that falsely accuse your good conversation in Christ."

What About Colossians Chapter 2, Verse 16?

Colossians Ch.2, V. 16

Let no man judge you in meat, or in drink, or respect of an holyday, or of the new moon, or of the sabbaths . . ."

There are more than one kind of sabbath referred to in the Holy Bible. There is the seventh day sabbath as has been discussed thus far and there are other sabbaths and holydays. These other sabbaths and holydays are what is referred to in Colossians Chapter 2, Verse 16. These sabbaths included the Passover, feast days, and some other holydays observed by the Jews. Among these days was The Dedication Of The Temple built by Solomon.

John Ch.10, Vs. 22-23
"And it was at Jerusalem the feast of the dedication, and it was winter. And Jesus walked in the temple in Solomon's porch."

Another such sabbath day is referred to in John Chapter 19, Verse 31.

John Ch.19, V. 31
"The Jews therefore, because it was the preparation, that the bodies should not remain upon the cross on the sabbath day, (for that sabbath was an high day,) . . ."

The lack of understanding of the above scripture is how the Pope of 325 A.D. has been able to deceive the people in celebrating the worship of the Spring goddess. This is the Easter celebration. Refer to our book, "Jesus Was Not Crucified When As Has Been Taught."

Here are some of the scriptures referring to the other sabbaths: Leviticus Ch.19, Vs. 1-3; Leviticus Ch.19, V. 30; Leviticus Ch.16, Vs. 29-31; Leviticus Ch.25, Vs. 1-5; Leviticus Ch.26, Vs. 27-35; Leviticus Ch.23, Vs. 4-7; Leviticus Ch.23, Vs. 15, 21, 23-28, 32-36 & 38-39; I Kings Ch.8, Vs. 63-66; etc.

These are the ordinances that Jesus blotted out, even nailing to them the cross.

SPECIAL EXCEPTIONS TO WORKING ON THE SABBATH:

People who try to get around the word of God concerning not working on the Sabbath, try to use certain instances when JESUS said it was alright to do certain things on the Sabbath. They point to the scriptures when JESUS' disciples were hungry and they plucked corn on the Sabbath. They, also, refer to the scriptures when JESUS healed on the Sabbath; the Pharisees complained that JESUS was working on the Sabbath.

EXPLANATION:

JESUS indicates his justification for the efforts on the Sabbath by two short statements.

1. 1.   In The Plucking Of Corn On The Sabbath—
2.   JESUS says—

("The sabbath was made for man, and not man for the sabbath.")

JESUS does not want or require anyone to starve because it is the Sabbath. Refer to Mark Ch. 2, Vs. 23-28.

Mark Ch. 2, Vs. 23-25&27

"And it came to pass, that he went through the corn fields on the sabbath day: and his disciples began, as they went, to pluck the ears of corn. And the Pharisees said unto him, Behold, why do they on the sabbath day that which is unlawful? And he said unto them, Have ye never read what David did, when he had need, and was a hungred, he, and they that were with him? How he went into the house of God in the days of Abiathar the high priest, and did eat showbread, which is not lawful to eat but for the priest, and gave also to them which were with him? And he said unto them, The sabbath was made for man, and not man for the sabbath.

1.   2.   In The Healing On The Sabbath—
2.   JESUS Indicates—

(It is right to do good on the sabbath.)

During the work of God is always permitted, even on the Sabbath. Refer to Luke Ch. 13, Vs. 14,15&16.

Luke Ch. 13, Vs. 14,15&16

"And the ruler of the synagogue answer with indignation, because that Jesus had healed on the Sabbath day, and said unto the people, There are six days in which men ought to work: in them therefore come and be healed, and not sabbath day. The Lord then answered him, and said, Thou hypocrite, doth not each one of you on the sabbath loose his ox or his ass from the stall, and lead him away to watering? And ought not this woman, being a daughter of Abraham, whom Satan hath bound, lo these eighteen years, be loosed from this bond on the sabbath day?"

If there is an emergency or critical need that happens the day of the Sabbath, JESUS does not expect you to ignore it. JESUS does not expect you to let someone suffer or die because it is the Sabbath. This does not include other regularly scheduled jobs or occupations on the Sabbath to meet your family needs. Ministering is always permitted, even on the Sabbath. Except for the above, the work that is not permitted on the Sabbath is work that you do on the six other days of the week.

THE FOUR EASY STEPS TO GET SAVED/BORN AGAIN:

1. Repent:

    a. ask God to forgive your sins, ask in the name of Jesus;
    b. surrender your will for God's will to be done in your life.

2. Ask God to save you, to fill you with the Holy Ghost, ask in the name of Jesus.

3. Do not ask God anymore to save you, just thank God, praise God for saving you. You must thank God in the name of Jesus. At the point of your greatest sincerity, you will speak in another language. This will be your sign of confirmation. God will be using your mouth to speak a language spoken somewhere on earth that you have not learned. This is your sign that you are born of the Spirit.

4. Get baptized in the name of Jesus Christ.

John Ch.3,Vs.3&5
"Jesus answered . . . Except a man be born again, he cannot see the kingdom of God . . . Jesus answered . . . Except a man be born of water and of the Spirit he cannot enter into the kingdom of God."

John Ch.3,V.8
". . . thou hearest the sound thereof . . . so is everyone that is born of the Spirit."

Colossians Ch.3,V.17
"And whatsoever ye do in word or deed, do all in the name of the Lord Jesus . . ."

CONTACT PAGE

We provide this page for those of you who desire to get in contact with us regarding:

    I. Ministering

        A. Preaching
        B. Singing
        C. Being prayed for

    II. Ordering tapes

        A. Audio of this book
        B. Preaching
        C. Singing
        D. Additional end times prophecies

    III. Ordering books
    IV. Questions concerning our next book
    V. Other questions.

Remember to give your address. For a quicker response, provide a telephone number where you can be reached.

Frederick & Sylvia Franklin's Ministry for JESUS
2669 Meadowview Drive
Mobile, AL, 36695
Telephone #: (251) 644-4329

ABOUT THE AUTHOR

"THE FINAL EXODUS" was written by Apostle Frederick E. Franklin of the ministry of F & SF Ministry For JESUS. What has been written is revelation from God that has been given to Frederick and his wife Sylvia. Frederick E. Franklin is an apostle, prophet and end times preacher. His wife, Sylvia Franklin, is a prophetess, evangelist and singer. The ministry positions stated above are what God, himself, has said/ordained and anointed them to be. Frederick and Sylvia have three children, Elijah Jeremiah Ezekiel Franklin, Daniel Isaiah Franklin, and Rebekah Anna Franklin. Frederick E. Franklin was a successful electrical engineer in private industry, state and federal government and also self-employment, before he was born again and told by God to preach.